flavours of
PRINCE EDWARD ISLAND

flavours of PRINCE EDWARD ISLAND
a culinary journey

∾ JEFF MCCOURT, ALLAN WILLIAMS & AUSTIN CLEMENT ∾

foreword by **chef michael smith**

photography by **james ingram** · *recipes provided by* **the PEI association of chefs and cooks**

whitecap

Published in 2010 by Whitecap Books

Whitecap Books is known for its expertise in the cookbook market and has produced some of the most innovative and familiar titles found in kitchens across North America. Visit our website at www.whitecap.ca.

Text copyright © 2010 PEI Association of Chefs and Cooks
Photography copyright © 2010 James Ingram
Design copyright © 2010 Whitecap Books

EDITING BY Lesley Cameron and Grace Yaginuma
DESIGN BY Mauve Pagé
PHOTOGRAPHY BY James Ingram except pages v, 91 and 92 by Berni Wood
FOOD STYLING AND PROP STYLING BY Patti Hetherington

Printed in China

LIBRARY AND ARCHIVES CANADA CATALOGUING IN PUBLICATION

McCourt, Jeff, 1971–
    Flavours of Prince Edward Island : a culinary journey / Jeff McCourt, Allan Williams, Austin Clement.

ISBN 978-1-77050-009-9

    1. Cookery, Canadian—Prince Edward Island style. 2. Cookery—Prince Edward Island. I. Williams, Allan, 1972– II. Clement, Austin, 1971– III. Title.

TX715.6.M325 2010   641.59717   C2009-906419-7

The publisher acknowledges the financial support of the Government of Canada through the Canada Book Fund (CBF) and the Province of British Columbia through the Book Publishing Tax Credit.

10 11 12 13 14   5 4 3 2 1

*To our wives—*GRACE, JODY *and* TREENA
—thanks for your patience. And to our kids—
FINN *and* MOLLY, MACKENZIE *and*
MATTHEW, EMMA *and* MADISON—
thanks for being our biggest fans!

contents

foreword

Prince Edward Island is a giant green farm, floating in the deep blue sea, surrounded by sandy beaches, rich with fertile soil and blessed with a community of passionate culinary artisans who make our local food so special.

I am deeply proud to be an Islander, and I am forever thankful for the soulful effect that life on Prince Edward Island has had on my understanding of food. It is here that I learned the most powerful lesson that any cook can learn: food is about more than just flavour, it is about people. That message is the essence of this beautiful book.

As a young chef, I came to Prince Edward Island to meet farmers and fishers, but I had no idea what that truly meant. Then I began driving up and down the long red clay lanes that lead to our farms, I waded into the surf with an oyster rake, held organic soil in my hands, spotted golden chanterelles hiding in the woods and downed shots of rum on the heaving deck of a lobster boat at sea. Gradually, it dawned on me that food is at its best when we taste its flavours *and* its stories.

Global food trends are returning to local food connections, yet here on Prince Edward Island, we've never had to leave. Our friends get up early in the morning and get their hands dirty producing food for our communities. Each year, we eagerly anticipate our first lobster feed, our first juicy strawberries, our first bite of fresh corn and the first drop of juice from a crisp apple just plucked from the tree. Islanders are blessed to know the people that produce our uniquely local and globally special food. With this book, you can get to know our food-producing community, too.

I have been friends with the chef-authors Jeff, Allan and Austin for a long time. We are more than just companions and colleagues, we are proud Islanders, and they have made me even more proud with their collective efforts to produce this magical book. These pages do more than just capture the essence of who most Islanders are, they inspire me to be even better. For that, I am thankful.

Chef Michael Smith
Bay Fortune, Prince Edward Island

Prince Edward Island is a chefs' paradise. An abundance of quality seasonal ingredients makes our task of presenting creative and flavourful dishes very easy. We chefs have a wonderful time sourcing our favourite ingredients directly from fishers and farmers—ingredients that come from the bounty of the sea, with its lobsters, mussels and oysters, and from the bounty of the land, with its potatoes, blueberries, beef and pork. From getting down to the wharf early in the morning to get our pick of the best female lobsters, to taking an afternoon to forage for the elusive chanterelle, finding top-quality ingredients is an incredible treat on this Island of ours!

beef

an island tradition

Beef farming on Prince Edward Island has been a way of life for generations. In times past, cattle were not only a source of milk and meat, but they were also the power that pulled the plough. They were genuinely indispensable.

PEI's rich soil provides the nutritious grasses for the cattle to graze on during the summer and the grains and corn needed for winter. Although many family farms have left the past behind and adopted more modern farming methods, there are still plenty of young farmers who are staying faithful to the tradition of raising wholesome, high-quality beef. You would be hard-pressed to drive 10 minutes in any direction without happening upon a beef farmer. Many of them work closely with our Island chefs to ensure that only top-quality ingredients make it to their tables. Sometimes the trip from the farm to the plate involves nothing more than crossing the yard!

On one of these farms, the Lewis farm, are some of the largest cattle I have ever seen. Chad Lewis raises purebred Charolais cattle that he sells for breeding. Great breeding is the real secret behind great beef. Many breeds of cattle are raised on PEI, and each has its own characteristics that contribute to the quality of the steak on your plate. Chad's Charolais cattle bring their impressive size and muscle tone to the mix, while the famous Angus breed brings fantastic marbling and tenderness. Some other well-known breeds raised here include Simmental, Hereford, Shorthorn and Limousin. Crossing some Angus and Charolais with just enough Simmental will give you great-tasting, tender beef. Farmers need to be patient, though. It can take up to two years for a cow to grow to market size, and during those two years an average cow will gain just 3 pounds (1.5 kg) a day.

Another essential ingredient for quality beef is the cattle's environment. At the Lewis farm the cattle graze on grasses as much as possible during the summer. The herd hangs out around its own pond, and there is ample shelter thanks to large barns and the odd lean-to in the fields. Also, antibiotics and steroids just aren't part of the picture here, making the beef wholesome and natural. From a chef's perspective, this is a huge bonus.

Here on the east coast we seem to like our portions a little smaller and with a natural, wholesome flavour. When farmers like Chad Lewis get it right, our butchers have prime wholesale cuts that are a bit smaller than our western counterparts', making it easier to cut thicker steaks and smaller roasts to suit our Island tastes. For example, I often find that if I want to cut an 8-ounce New York strip loin from western beef, I'm left with a thin sliver of meat that is too thin to cook in any way but well done. The same weight of strip steak from Island beef will be a smaller but thicker piece of meat, and so it's easier to cook. So, ask yourself, do you like your steak thick and juicy or thin and dry?

Do we chefs have a secret source for these ingredients? We sure do. The Riverview Market in Charlottetown is a perfect example of all things Island and all things fresh. If you're looking for a chef, this is where you will find us shopping. You walk into the market and you find yourself surrounded by every type of produce and meat product that our Island farms have to offer. I usually spend my time speaking with the butchers or selecting my beef from the walk-in cooler. There is just something about meat hanging in a cooler that gets me excited about cooking!

It is important to me to know where my beef comes from. If you ask the butchers, they can tell you from what farm, in what county. Things are done the old-fashioned way here. The beef is dry-aged for at least 14 days (usually more), and every piece is trimmed by hand. I can pick out my piece and watch the butchers cut my steaks the way I want them. The rest is left up to the chef.

old-fashioned pot roast

This recipe is an old favourite, and it's especially great because you don't have to spend a fortune on the meat. Choose tougher cuts from the leg or shoulder, and let the slow, moist heat do all the work. The liquid that is left after roasting carries huge flavour and makes a great gravy to serve with the meat. SERVES 4—6

1 Tbsp (15 mL) vegetable oil
3 lb (1.5 kg) boneless beef chuck arm roast
   (blade or shoulder pot roast)
1 tsp (5 mL) salt
1 Tbsp (15 mL) freshly cracked black pepper
1 lb (500 g) white button mushrooms
   (halved)
3 large cloves garlic (minced)
2 medium onions (chopped)
2 cups (500 mL) hot beef stock
   (page 242)
¼ cup (60 mL) balsamic vinegar
1 bay leaf

Heat the oil in a Dutch oven or covered roasting pan over medium heat until smoking hot.

Add the beef and brown on all sides. Remove from the pot, season with salt and pepper and set aside.

Add the mushrooms, garlic and onions to the Dutch oven. Cook, stirring, until the onion is lightly browned. Add the stock, balsamic vinegar and bay leaf. Bring to a simmer, then add the beef. There's no need to stir at this stage.

Return the roast to the pot, reduce the heat, cover tightly and simmer for about 1½ hours. Turn the roast over and simmer until the roast is fork-tender, another hour.

Remove the beef from the Dutch oven, cover with foil and keep warm in the oven. Discard the bay leaf. Reduce the liquid to a gravy consistency and serve with the roast.

Serve this with mashed potatoes and roasted root vegetables.

using the right cut

If you want to make the most of beef when you're cooking, you need to understand a few basics. Too often what could have been a great meal is spoiled because the wrong cut of meat was used.

The muscles that are used the most—that is, the leg and shoulder muscles—produce the toughest cuts. These include inside or outside round, eye of round, cross rib, blade and shoulder roasts. These cost less than other cuts, but they have a lot of connective tissue and so they require marinating or a moist slow-cooking method such as stewing, simmering or braising to become tender; they're also often ground. The most tender cuts are found on the loin where the muscles are not used as much and have less connective tissue. Common cuts from the loin include rib eye, New York strip, tenderloin, T-bone and sirloin. They're also the most expensive cuts. They're great for dry cooking methods such as roasting, grilling and sautéing,

and they don't need to be marinated for tenderness, although they do benefit from added flavour. The easiest way to add flavour is to simply remove or reduce the acidic ingredients from your favourite marinade.

Another consideration is fat content. Usually we see fat as the bad guy, but in the case of meat it's the flavour builder. Cuts like prime rib or shoulder roast have great flavour because of their high fat content. Leaner cuts like beef tenderloin are very tender but have no "beefy" flavour of their own. They require some flavour building. That's why chefs serve a big-flavoured sauce alongside beef tenderloin.

You should now have enough information to ask your butcher all the right questions. In time, and with experience, you will be able to look at the cooking methods in a recipe and determine for yourself what cut will work best.

easter beef stew with red wine and roasted root vegetables

There is no comfort food like a good stew. In the past these hearty meals were often made from anything that the farmers could not sell. Today when we make stew, we still use the cheaper options, but that does not reduce their flavour—or their value—in any way. Serve this with some crusty bread and hot tea, and the cold will just melt away. SERVES 4—6

STEW

3 Tbsp (45 mL) canola oil

3 lb (1.5 kg) stewing meat (large dice)

3 lb (1.5 kg) Yukon Gold potatoes (peeled, medium dice)

1 lb (500 g) white button mushrooms (quartered)

2 medium red onions (small dice)

1 red bell pepper (small dice)

2 Tbsp (30 mL) chopped garlic

¼ cup (60 mL) chopped fresh rosemary

2 cups (500 mL) red wine

8 cups (2 L) hot beef stock (page 242)

ROASTED ROOT VEGETABLES

2 medium parsnips (peeled, medium dice)

2 medium carrots (peeled, medium dice)

½ medium turnip (peeled, medium dice)

½ medium butternut squash (peeled, medium dice)

¼ cup (60 mL) chopped assorted fresh herbs (your preference)

vegetable spice blend

salt and pepper

extra virgin olive oil

For the stew, preheat a large stew pot with oil and sear the beef until it turns a rich brown colour. Remove the meat from the pot and add the potatoes, button mushrooms, red onions, bell pepper and garlic. Sauté for 3 to 4 minutes until the onions are translucent.

Return the meat to the pot and stir in the chopped rosemary. Deglaze with the red wine, reducing the liquid by half. Add the beef stock and bring to a boil. Reduce the heat and simmer, uncovered, until the potatoes are just cooked through.

Adjust the seasoning of the stew as it cooks. Simmer for about 1 hour, then remove the beef from the pot. Reduce the liquid by half, season to taste and return the beef to the pot. Keep hot until the root vegetables are ready.

Meanwhile, prepare the root vegetables.

Preheat the oven to 350°F (180°C). Line a baking sheet with parchment paper.

Place the parsnips, carrots, turnip, butternut squash, fresh herbs, spice blend and salt and pepper in a large mixing bowl and toss with enough olive oil to coat everything evenly. Transfer the vegetables to the prepared baking sheet. Roast the vegetables for 20 to 30 minutes. Add to the stew before serving and toss well.

Serve this dish family-style—that is, place the stew in the middle of the table and let everyone help themselves!

One of my great memories is of the boxes of beef we used to get for the winter when I was young. We lived next door to a beef farm, and every year we would split a side of beef with another family. Usually two or three boxes would arrive, and we would pick through them piece by piece. Each cut would be wrapped in brown paper or plastic and labelled. Roasts were stored in one side of the freezer, stewing beef in another. There was always lots of ground beef that we would mix in big bowls with Dad's spices and let sit for a few hours. We would reconvene after the flavours had had time to set and start making perfect burger patties for the winter. We froze them between layers of wax paper and wrapped them tightly in plastic. The next night was always stew night, and the Easter Beef Stew recipe is a great example of how best to use a tougher cut of meat by slowly stewing it until it is super-tender. The red wine adds real depth and a taste of the Old World, and the root vegetables are ones you can easily get all winter long.

marinated east coast cowboy steak with warm sour cream potato salad

This classic meat-and-potatoes dish steals the show on barbecue days. When you want to impress, this is the one to bring out. "Cowboy steak" refers to a rib steak with the bone in, but you can use a boneless rib eye if you prefer. This recipe works well with strip loin, sirloin or any other grilling steak. Just remember that a rib eye is fatty, so beware of flare-ups. Also, rib eye takes longer to cook than leaner meats. SERVES 4–6

MARINADE

1 cup (250 mL) balsamic vinegar
½ cup (125 mL) brown sugar (packed)
salt and pepper
¼ cup (60 mL) maple syrup
3 Tbsp (45 mL) chopped fresh oregano
1 bay leaf
2 Tbsp (30 mL) minced garlic
dash Tabasco sauce

STEAK
four 12 oz (375 g) rib eye steaks (bone in)

POTATO SALAD

3 lb (1.5 kg) baby red potatoes (boiled, cooled, cut into wedges)
1 medium red onion (quartered, sliced)
1 bunch chives (snipped)
1 red bell pepper (thinly sliced)
1 green bell pepper (thinly sliced)
2 Tbsp (30 mL) Dijon mustard
2 cups (500 mL) sour cream
Tabasco sauce
salt and pepper
1 cup (250 mL) bacon bits (optional)

Place all the marinade ingredients in a large bowl. Whisk until they are well combined, and season to taste.

Place the 4 steaks in the marinade for 1 hour while you assemble the potato salad. When the potato salad is ready, the steaks should be cooked to order on a preheated grill for the best results.

For the potato salad, make sure the potatoes have cooled completely before you begin. This allows the starches to relax so that the potatoes will not be as sticky or difficult to handle. Fold the potatoes, onion, chives and bell peppers together in a large mixing bowl. Add the Dijon, sour cream, and Tabasco to taste and gently fold together to coat everything evenly. Season to taste and add the bacon bits (if desired).

grilled PEI beef kabobs with garlic and thyme vinaigrette

These kabobs are great because you can make them up ahead of time and pull them out when you're ready to cook them. If you have any friends who like their meat well done, you can partly grill the meat before you assemble the kabobs. That way you won't burn the veggies. These are great with roasted or grilled potatoes and corn on the cob. SERVES 4—6

BEEF KABOBS
**eight 6-inch (15 cm) bamboo
  or metal skewers
3 lb (1.5 kg) sirloin roast (cut in 1-inch/
  2.5 cm cubes)
1 medium red onion (large dice)
16 white button mushrooms (cleaned
  and left whole)
1 red bell pepper (large dice)
1 green bell pepper (large dice)**

VINAIGRETTE
**1¼ cups (310 mL) extra virgin olive oil
¾ cup (185 mL) white wine vinegar
2 Tbsp (30 mL) roasted and minced garlic
¼ cup (60 mL) chopped fresh thyme
1 Tbsp (15 mL) Dijon mustard
salt and pepper**

If using bamboo skewers, soak them in water for 1 hour. Making sure your skewers are thoroughly soaked will minimize the risk of burning, flare-ups and splintering. Also, do all your cutting and prepping before you begin to assemble the kabobs to make things easier for yourself.

First, prepare the vinaigrette. Place all the vinaigrette ingredients in a large bowl, whisk until well combined and then adjust seasoning to taste.

To assemble the kabobs, place a cube of beef onto a skewer, then add the other ingredients in succession. Be sure to have a cube of beef at either end of the skewer and in the middle. Place the kabobs in the vinaigrette to marinate for 15 minutes to 2 hours.

Preheat the grill on medium-high heat.

Grill the kabobs to the desired doneness.

= tip =
If the vinaigrette is too oily, add vinegar; if too acidic, add more oil.

When I was a teenager, my friends and I spent a lot of time sitting on my friend Walter's (a.k.a. Mick's) deck, enjoying the view over Shaw's Bay and indulging in some great food. Over the years a lot of food was eaten at Mick's Marina, as his place became known. Mick was a great host, but for some reason the cooking always seemed to fall at least partly to me. One day in particular stands out, a day we had been out water-skiing. When we returned, we found a basket of food on the deck for us—some beef, peppers, onions and mushrooms. (It was like Christmas come early for me!) Mick and I went to work making a marinade and putting together some beef kabobs that we threw on the grill. They were fantastic. That day I realized that great food doesn't always need loads of planning and prepping. You just need some great ingredients, and great friends. To this day, whenever I've been out all day in the summer, like at the beach and getting really baked by the sun, I find myself throwing together some beef kabobs and relaxing on the deck. You may even find Mick here if you time it right . . .

pork

naturally delicious

Few meals feel as familiar and comforting as a Sunday pork roast with all the trimmings. I've always loved pork. It's one of the most versatile meats for a chef because of all the different cuts and all the ways you can prepare it. If you know what you're doing, you can use just about any part of the pig to prepare something wonderful.

The loin cuts such as rib chops, pork loin roasts or tenderloin are the easiest to prepare but the most expensive to purchase. The real challenge is to prepare something brilliant at half the cost. But it's entirely possible. The belly, for example, is perfect for making your own bacon or for slowly braising in maple syrup or stock. The shoulder makes a perfect pot roast and holds a ton of flavours. The legs are great for hams or stews, and all the scrap meat is perfect for grinding up for a meat pie, stuffing or even sausages. When purchasing pork from your butcher, take the time to talk to him or her about selecting the best cut for what you plan to make. It would be a shame to purchase a quality pork loin only to cut it up for stew.

Many of PEI's larger pork operations of a generation ago have closed down and given way to a new breed of farmer. These farmers have looked further back and learned the old craft of raising healthier, more flavourful hogs using Old World breeds and organic or more traditional farming methods. This way of thinking is beautifully in tune with the vision of Island chefs to offer a local, more environmentally responsible cuisine. Prince Edward Island pork has its own flavour that marries well with the tastes of our Island, from fresh berries, fruit and vegetables in the spring and early summer, to the cranberries and tree fruit that will make jams, jellies and preserves to be served alongside the chops, roasts and stews all winter long.

Producing high-quality pork involves good breeding practices, quality feed and loads of time and patience. It takes about six months for a hog to reach market from the time it is born. This past summer I visited the hog farm one of my pals grew up on. As kids, we spent a lot of time working in the barns around the pigs and learning a lot about where pork really comes from. At that time the farm, which is located in Harrington, just a few miles from the north-shore beaches of Brackley, was owned by Chris Linzel, but it's now owned by the Artz family from the Netherlands. The ownership may have changed, but it's pretty much the same as I

remember. The long driveway where Mark and I used to race our go-carts leads to the same old farmhouse at the top of the hill, and the whole farm is surrounded by fields of 8-foot-tall corn as far as you can see. When I opened the car door the smell was the same as 25 years ago, and it instantly took me back to my childhood. It's that "country" smell that you don't really like but that somehow makes the air feel fresher and unpolluted.

The Artz farm raises about 15,000 hogs, most of which are exported to Quebec. During a two-hour visit I met three generations of the Artz family, right down to two-year-old Anthony, who was proud to show me his piglet that was born during the night. Perhaps he is the next generation of farmer and will carry on the traditions of his father and grandfather, providing great PEI pork for years to come.

PEI barbecue pulled-pork sandwich

*This sandwich is a sweet and sticky example of how
Island pork and a few ingredients you probably
already have in the kitchen can combine to create
something unforgettable. What is great about this dish
is that it can be prepared a day ahead and kept in
the refrigerator until you need it. Try changing up the
flavours a bit by substituting the barbecue sauce. For a
more Asian flair replace the balsamic and smoke with
an equivalent volume of soy sauce, garlic and ginger.
Always make way more sauce than you need so that
you can use it on everything you eat for days after the
meat is gone.* SERVES 6

PORK

3 lb (1.5 kg) boneless pork shoulder
salt and pepper
2 large Spanish onions (medium slices)
1 head garlic (chopped)

BARBECUE SAUCE

6 cups (1.5 L) ketchup
2 cups (500 mL) balsamic vinegar
2 cups (500 mL) brown sugar (packed)
1 cup (250 mL) diced onion
¼ cup (60 mL) hickory smoke seasoning
2 Tbsp (30 mL) minced garlic
1 Tbsp (15 mL) Worcestershire sauce
2 tsp (10 mL) Tabasco sauce
salt and pepper

Preheat the oven to 400°F (200°C).

Season the pork shoulder with salt and pepper.
Place the onions and garlic in a roasting pan and
sit the pork shoulder on top. Roast in the oven for
30 minutes to brown the pork and vegetables.

Meanwhile, mix all the sauce ingredients
together in a large mixing bowl. Adjust the seasoning
to taste. Keep refrigerated until needed.

Reduce the oven temperature to 300°F (150°C).

Pour the barbecue sauce over the browned pork
shoulder, cover tightly with foil and return to the
oven for 2 hours to slowly braise in the sauce. The
roast is finished when it is tender and reaches an
internal temperature of 180°F (82°C). (Use a meat
thermometer to check.) The meat should pull apart
with little or no resistance.

Allow the pork to cool, still covered in foil, in the
sauce, until you can handle it comfortably. Remove
it from the sauce and pull it apart into pieces. Mix
the pork pieces back into the sauce and gently reheat
in the oven.

To serve, place the pulled meat mixture on a fresh
baguette or toasted kaiser, or roll in a soft tortilla
wrap. If you don't want it as a sandwich, it is great
with some mashed potatoes and grilled vegetables.
You may need to remove any excess sauce.

hearty braised pork with onion pan gravy

Recipes like this braised pork are the type of meal that would have been served at dinner to the Linzel family when they came in from the barns. The gravy was rich and thick, and mustard pickles would have been brought out from the cellar.

Pork shoulder is perfect for this. It has a good amount of fat, which will add loads of flavour, and the cost of shoulder cuts is relatively low. If you like, you can add some small roasting potatoes during the last hour of cooking. If you're too impatient to wait for the gravy to reduce, just thicken it with a bit of flour or cornstarch mixed with some cold water. SERVES 4—6

BRAISED PORK

3 lb (1.5 kg) boneless pork shoulder
salt and pepper
2 small Spanish onions (sliced)
1 head garlic (small dice)
1 large carrot (medium-sliced on a bias)
1 Tbsp (15 mL) Pommery mustard
1 Tbsp (15 mL) Dijon mustard
1 cup (250 mL) dry red wine
4 cups (1 L) hot pork stock (chicken
   stock, page 243, also works here)

ONION PAN GRAVY

2 Tbsp (30 mL) olive oil
1 large Spanish onion (medium slices)
4 cloves garlic (minced)
1 cup (250 mL) dry red wine
4 cups (1 L) reserved braising liquid
salt and pepper

Preheat the oven to 400°F (200°C).

Season the pork shoulder with salt and pepper. Place the onions, garlic and carrot in a roasting pan and sit the pork shoulder on top. Roast in the oven for 30 minutes to brown the pork and vegetables.

Blend together the mustards and spread all over the roast. Transfer to the stovetop. Add the red wine, allow the wine to reduce slightly, then add the pork stock.

Reduce the oven temperature to 350°F (180°C).

Cover the roast tightly with foil and roast for 2 hours to slowly braise. The roast is finished when it is tender and reaches an internal temperature of 180°F (82°C). (Use a meat thermometer to check.) The meat should pull apart with little or no resistance. Remove the meat to a platter, reserving the braising liquid.

For the gravy, preheat a skillet, then add the olive oil and sauté the onion until brown. Add the minced garlic. Deglaze with the red wine, allow the liquid to reduce by half, then add the 4 cups (1 L) of reserved braising liquid. Let the liquid reduce until it reaches the desired thickness.

Homemade bread and molasses could be served alongside. And mustard pickles (page 162) and beets would usually make this family meal complete.

---

tip

Pommery mustard is a French-style grainy mustard. It is available at most specialty food shops and in the ethnic section of most supermarkets.

Riverview Market in Charlottetown is just a couple of miles from the school and provides high-quality meats and produce to the more locally minded restaurants in the city. The market was created by four farming families as a way to provide wholesome farm goods produced using traditional farming methods. Farming, although frequently perceived as being very romantic, is actually a tough business, and many Island farmers find it difficult to make ends meet. These four families realized they had to take a different approach to how they sold their goods. One is a vegetable grower, another a beef farmer, another a poultry farmer and the fourth a pork producer.

The butchers at Riverview are passionate about meat and meat products. They smoke their own hams, make amazing artisan bacons and supply fresh and smoked sausages to many of the local restaurants and backyard barbecuers. The pork sold in the market comes only from Kenny Mutch's pork operation, which uses no growth hormones, steroids or animal-based feeds. I know Kenny well and understand his passion and attention to detail when raising his hogs. He talks about his farm the same way a proud chef talks about a favourite dish. Kenny is a breeding expert who raises Landrace, Yorkshire and Duroc hogs on Top Line Swine, his 150-year-old farm (in Earnscliffe). I use his Duroc pork because I like its increased amount of marbling in the muscle and great flavour. Compared with most other pork, it is a darker meat, but it looks very similar after it is cooked. You really notice the difference when you cure and smoke Duroc into ham. Once again I find myself addicted to another local food that you can find only on PEI. I do live in a chefs' paradise.

smoked island pork tenderloin with maple syrup and apples

Pork tenderloin is the most tender cut of pork you can buy. It's also very lean, which makes it a great choice for those of you watching your waistline. Quite often you'll find smoked items paired with a sweet partner on a plate. Here we use apples and maple syrup to balance the pork. It is important not to overcook the pork or it will become dry. SERVES 4

12 cups (3 L) mesquite or cedar
   smoking chips
two 1¼ lb (625 g) pork tenderloins
salt and pepper
2 Tbsp (30 mL) olive oil
3 Tbsp (45 mL) chopped green onion
1 Tbsp (15 mL) chopped garlic
2 medium McIntosh apples (cored,
   quartered, sliced)
1 cup (250 mL) dry white wine
2 cups (500 mL) maple syrup

Preheat the oven to 350°F (180°C).

Place the wood chips in a roasting pan and place a cooling rack over the wood chips. Moisten the wood chips and place the pan on the stovetop on medium-low heat (see tip on page 69). The smoke will start after 2 to 3 minutes.

Season the pork tenderloin with salt and pepper.

In a hot skillet add 1 Tbsp (15 mL) of the olive oil and sear the pork on all sides until it's a golden colour. Place the seared pork on the rack over the smoking wood chips, cover tightly with a lid or foil and place in the preheated oven for 20 minutes. The pork is done when it reaches an internal temperature of 150°F (65°C). (Use a meat thermometer to check.)

For the sauce, use the skillet from searing the pork to sauté the green onion and garlic in the remaining olive oil. Add the apple slices and continue to sauté until the green onion, garlic and apple slices are slightly brown. Deglaze the pan with the white wine. Reduce the liquid by half, then add the maple syrup and continue to reduce to form a glaze.

To serve, slice the pork into medallions, fan on a plate and drizzle the glaze over the smoked pork medallions. You can do this on a serving platter or on individual dishes, whichever suits the occasion best.

This dish goes great with pan-fried gnocchi or your favourite mashed potatoes.

tip

The pie can also be cooled completely and bagged and frozen for later. If frozen, allow to thaw before cooking in a 350°F (180°C) oven until golden brown and warmed through, 25 to 30 minutes.

acadian meat pie

This traditional Acadian meat pie is a staple in our freezer for around Christmas. I got this tried-and-true recipe passed on from my great-aunt Kay. It's excellent with chili sauce (see page 163). MAKES 2 PIES

FILLING
2.5 lb (1.25 kg) turkey thigh or breast
2 lb (1 kg) pork shoulder or butt roast
2 small potatoes (whole)
1 large onion (medium dice)
2 tsp (10 mL) chopped fresh summer savory
salt and pepper
cornstarch and water slurry (as needed
   to thicken)

CRUST
2 cups (500 mL) all-purpose flour
salt
1½ tsp (7.5 mL) baking powder
½ cup (125 mL) vegetable shortening
½ cup (125 mL) 2% milk
¼ cup (60 mL) cooled meat broth
   (from the cooking of the meat)
1 egg (beaten) + 1 tsp (5 mL) water
   for brushing

Dampen two 10-inch (25 cm) pie plates with water.

For the filling, bring the meat to a boil in a large stockpot with just enough water to cover and simmer until the meat begins to tenderize, about 45 minutes.

Add the potatoes and onion for the final 25 minutes' cooking time. Using a slotted spoon, remove the meat, potatoes and onion from the pot and let cool. Shred the meat into small pieces, dice the potatoes into small cubes and combine them. Season well with the savory and salt and pepper and reserve. Over medium-high heat, reduce the cooking liquid by half. Thicken with the cornstarch slurry. Season to taste and cool. (You will be using ¼ cup/60 mL for the crust, and another ½ cup/120 mL for the filling.)

For the crust, combine the dry ingredients in a mixing bowl. Cut in the shortening until you have pea-sized crumbs. Combine the milk and ¼ cup (60 mL) of the broth and gradually add this liquid to the dry ingredients. Mix until the dough has a smooth consistency. Divide the dough into 4 pieces and roll out 2 double crusts. Place the bottom crusts in the prepared pie plates.

Preheat the oven to 350°F (180°C).

Divide the meat and potato mixture equally between the 2 pies. Add ¼ cup (60 mL) of cool broth to each pie and cover with the top crusts. Trim the edges and use your thumbs to flute the 2 crusts. Make a small steam hole in the centre by cutting out a small circle of dough.

Bake for 35 minutes. Brush the top of the pies with the beaten egg and water mix. Bake for another 15 minutes.

Let cool slightly before serving.

mussels

Steamed Mussels New London Style *p. 35* | Fried Mussels with Lemon Caper
Mayonnaise *p. 38* | Marinated Mussel Salad with Fennel and Citrus Vinaigrette *p. 41*

island gold

Prince Edward Island is a world leader in the mussel industry. Many years ago mussels were only harvested wild, but modern methods of rope culturing or farming mussels mean that the Island offers a product that is actually greatly superior to the wild product. The mussels are suspended from ropes, so they won't touch the sandy bottom of the ocean. And the bays where they are grown are carefully selected based on salinity and the amount of natural feed in the water, producing something with a good growth rate and no grit.

When the waters begin to warm in the spring and early summer, female mussels release eggs into the water and male mussels release sperm. The fertilized eggs form into larvae, also known as spat. Spat begin life around $1/16$ inch (1.5 mm) in size, moving through the water with the tides and currents for a couple of weeks in search of something to cling onto. Once they have found their home, they filter water through their digestive system and nourish themselves on the natural plankton and algae. (Apparently a large mussel can filter up to 15 gallons/ 60 litres every day.)

The spat are then placed in "socks." A sock is basically a slender mesh bag that contains the mussels and allows them to feed and grow. They range from 6 to 12 feet (1.8 to 3.6 metres) in length and are placed 2 to 3 feet (0.6 to 0.9 metres) apart. Once the socks are filled, they are tied to long lines of buoys that are anchored at each end and run parallel across the bodies of water. As the mussels grow and gain weight, the mussel farmers will tie more buoys to the lines to keep them up off the sandy bottom.

The waters off Prince Edward Island freeze in the winter to a thickness of 4 feet (1.2 metres). This ice will move with the tides and cause incredible damage if it comes in contact with the mussels and/or mussel lines. To prevent this from happening, the fishers have to remove the buoys from the long lines and allow the lines to sit about 6 feet (1.8 metres) below the surface. The mussel socks will be left to grow for 18 to 24 months before being harvested.

It would be so simple if the fishers could just hang the socks in the water and come back 18 months later to harvest, but this is not the case. Once mussels have been in one place for a long time they seem to get comfortable and their growth slows down. Fishers periodically lift the lines out of the water, remove any starfish (a natural predator) and spray the mussels with salt water. This wakes up the mussels and stimulates growth.

Working in food product development has given me the opportunity to work directly with many food companies to promote their products locally, nationally and internationally. I've noticed something during this time. Yes, some people do not like shellfish at all, while others absolutely love it. But there's a third group of people: the ones who have never tried it. This group is usually unsure of how to prepare shellfish, which may have contributed to their initial reluctance. But shellfish doesn't have to be complicated. In fact, many recipes in this chapter are quite simple and are a good starting point. Beginners to shellfish should try out dishes with ingredients that don't overpower the taste of the main ingredient—the classic steamed mussel with a little wine, aromatics and herbs is a great example. Once you have mastered this recipe and its variations, why not try some of the others?

Mussels are very nutritious. They contain omega-3s as well as calcium, iron, magnesium, zinc, potassium and vitamins A, B6 and B12. They are also low in both fat and cholesterol.

steamed mussels new london style

One of the simplest ways to prepare mussels is to steam them. To do this properly you must quickly bring the liquid to a boil and then add the mussels. Steam builds up under the lid and cooks the mussels—do not remove the lid for at least five minutes. If you are constantly removing the lid to check you will be reducing the amount of steam, and the whole thing will take longer to cook. SERVES 4—6

¼ cup (60 mL) finely diced onion
3 Tbsp (45 mL) diced celery
3 Tbsp (45 mL) minced garlic
2 Tbsp (30 mL) olive oil
½ cup (125 mL) dry white wine
4 lb (1.8 kg) Island Gold mussels (cleaned)
2 Tbsp (30 mL) chopped fresh parsley, tarragon and/or chives
2 Tbsp (30 mL) unsalted butter (softened)
salt and pepper

Heat a medium-sized pot to medium heat. Sauté the onion, celery and garlic in the olive oil until translu-cent, about 2 minutes. Increase the heat to high, add the white wine and bring to a boil. Add the mussels, cover and cook for another 6 minutes. Remove the mussels from the pot, transfer them to a warmed serving dish and set aside. Reduce the liquid by half to concentrate the flavours. Add the herbs, then whisk in the butter and season to taste with salt and pepper. Pour the sauce overtop the mussels to serve.

variations:
> Once the sauce is reduced by half, add 2 cups (500 mL) small diced tomatoes (canned are fine) before you add the herbs. Whisk in the butter and season to taste with salt and pepper.
OR
> Once the sauce is reduced by half, add ½ cup (125 mL) whipping cream. Return to a simmer and then add the herbs, whisk in the butter and season to taste with salt and pepper.

Whichever option you choose, serve with lots of crusty French bread for dipping.

buying and preparing mussels

When purchasing mussels, choose ones with a clean, sea-like aroma. Some people will tell you not to use any mussels that are open, but don't feel you always have to follow this advice. Mussels will open occasionally, a natural occurrence. If you find an open mussel, gently tap it. If it begins to close, it's fine; if it doesn't, discard it, as it is no longer alive.

To store fresh mussels, place them in a perforated pan on top of a solid pan, with space between the two pans to catch any drips. (The shelf life of the mussels will be shorter if the mussels are allowed to sit in their own juices.) Cover with damp towels and refrigerate until ready to use. The typical shelf life of a mussel is 12 to 14 days from the date that they leave the packaging plant, the date attached to the mesh bag that the mussels are sold in. If your fishmonger is selling mussels in bulk, you should be able to ask for the tag to see this harvest date.

To clean the mussels, rinse them with cold water just before use. There should not be any beards on the mussels, as they go through a cleaning process before hitting the stores. But if you do find a beard, simply pinch it between your thumb and forefinger and pull it towards the pointy end of the shell.

Orange mussel meat comes from female mussels,
white mussel meat from male mussels.

fried mussels with lemon caper mayonnaise

I know that many people worry about consuming deep-fried food, but I think moderation is the key. There is nothing wrong with eating it once in a while, especially when it tastes as good as this! Enjoy the crunch of the Japanese breadcrumbs and the sweet, salty taste of the Prince Edward Island mussel.

SERVES 6—8

LEMON CAPER MAYONNAISE
½ cup (125 mL) mayonnaise
2 Tbsp (30 mL) lemon juice
1 Tbsp (15 mL) capers (finely chopped)
1 Tbsp (15 mL) minced garlic
1 tsp (5 mL) lemon zest
salt and pepper

MUSSELS
½ cup (125 mL) dry white wine
½ cup (125 mL) finely diced onion
2 Tbsp (30 mL) minced garlic
4 lb (1.8 kg) mussels (cleaned)
½ cup (125 mL) all-purpose flour
½ tsp (2 mL) sea salt
1 Tbsp (15 mL) garlic powder
pinch cayenne pepper
1 cup (250 mL) egg wash (page 251)
2 cups (500 mL) breadcrumbs
   (Japanese panko preferred)
2 cups (500 mL) canola oil (for frying)
salt and pepper

For the lemon caper mayonnaise, simply combine all the mayonnaise ingredients, seasoning to taste with salt and pepper. This will keep for 1 week in the refrigerator.

For the mussels, bring the wine, onion and garlic to a simmer in a large pot. Add the mussels, then cover and cook until they are just opened, 4 to 6 minutes. Allow them to cool and remove them from their shells.

Combine the flour, salt, garlic powder and cayenne in a bowl. Toss the mussels in batches in this flour mixture until lightly coated. Shake off any excess flour, dip the coated mussels in egg wash and then toss in the breadcrumbs. Repeat until all the mussels are coated.

Heat the canola oil in a large pot until a candy thermometer shows 365°F (185°C).

Gently dip the mussels into the hot oil and allow them to cook until golden brown, 3 to 5 minutes. Fry them in batches to avoid overcrowding the pan. Drain on paper towel and season to taste with salt and pepper.

Serve the mussels with the mayonnaise on the side for dipping.

Prince Edward Island mussels are our very own "Island Gold." Over 38 million pounds (over 17 million kg) are harvested from the briny waters of PEI every year. Scenic coastal vistas often include the view of countless buoys marking the mussel socks hanging in the water below. Our cultured mussels are shipped worldwide and have even been spotted being advertised in restaurants in New York, Chicago and Tokyo!

marinated mussel salad with fennel and citrus vinaigrette

In this recipe the mussels are steamed, then cooled and marinated. Everyone I've made this for has greatly enjoyed it. It makes a wonderful appetizer or a main course—just increase the portion size. SERVES 4 AS A MAIN DISH, 8 AS AN APPETIZER

½ cup (125 mL) sliced white onion
¼ cup (60 mL) minced garlic
2 Tbsp (30 mL) olive oil
½ cup (125 mL) dry white wine
5 lb (2.2 kg) mussels (cleaned)
½ cup (125 mL) thinly sliced fennel
½ cup (125 mL) thinly sliced carrots
½ cup (125 mL) thinly sliced red bell pepper
½ cup (125 mL) thinly sliced green
   bell pepper
½ cup (125 mL) thinly sliced yellow
   bell pepper
¼ cup (60 mL) thinly sliced green onions

¼ cup (60 mL) chopped fresh basil
¼ cup (60 mL) chopped fresh parsley
2 Tbsp (30 mL) chopped fresh tarragon
1 Tbsp (15 mL) lemon zest
¾ cup (180 mL) citrus vinaigrette
   (page 246)
salt and pepper

In a medium-sized pot sauté the white onion and garlic in the olive oil over medium heat for 3 minutes. Add the white wine and mussels, cover and cook on high until the shells open, 5 to 7 minutes. Remove the mussels from the pot, allow them to cool and remove them from the shells.

Reduce the juice that is left in the pot by half. Cool and reserve. Toss the mussel meat, vegetables, herbs and lemon zest with 1 cup (250 mL) of the cooled cooking liquid. Add the citrus vinaigrette and season to taste with salt and pepper.

clams

buried treasure

Prince Edward Island's sandy shoreline is the perfect place for clams to hide. Buried like sunken treasure, they are somewhere in the soft red clay, waiting to play hide-and-go-seek. You don't need to take much along—a bucket, a small shovel, a plunger and some patience. Then you just start digging. At low tide, it's as simple as walking out on the flats to look for some holes in the sand. As with any treasure hunt, the reward is carting home a bucket of loot. In this case, the treasure can be steamed, baked or even deep-fried. Find a local Islander and he or she will have a dozen ways to cook up these morsels. Clams are simply part of the Island way of life.

You will find clams in just about every beach-front corner of the Island, but my favourite place is down east between Montague and Souris. It's where my summertime home base is, actually—my favourite restaurant, Clam Diggers, is located in Georgetown. My daughter Madison and I often find ourselves on the beach in front of the restaurant digging holes during low tide. Although she is not very interested in eating clams, she is always up for a good hunt. Going for a dig is a great way to spend time with someone special and get a little dinner at the same time. Just last week we spent the evening digging until the tide came in. We divided the loot and added it to our family clambake on the beach. In a world of video games, YouTube and the Internet, you can still have lots of fun digging for clams, and it's a great way to enjoy unspoiled Island culture.

The most common clam varieties you will find in PEI are the soft-shell clam (also known as squirt or steamer clams) and the medium-sized hard-shell quahogs. Razor clams, which get their name from their resemblance to a straight blade razor, are also found on the beaches, but they can be a bit more elusive. These three varieties are hunted directly on the beach during low tide. Locals say that clams run with the tidal moons and are more plentiful after a full moon.

Regardless of when you go digging, you need to know what to look for. If you're on the hunt for quahogs or steamers, look for little holes in the centre of small, shallow indents. These are the trademark signs of clams just below the surface; sometimes water will squirt straight out as you walk close to them—that's when you know you're in the right spot. With your finger, make the opening just a little bigger and position your plunger over the hole.

Plunge until the clam is pulled to the surface and the sand is forced away. If you don't have a plunger, use your shovel to dig a wide hole about 12 inches (30 cm) around to scoop the clam(s) out. You have to move quickly because the clams are trying to escape. Razor clams are even more fun because their arrival is more dramatic. With these clams, you're looking for small, round indents in the sand, about the size of a silver dollar. With the handle of your shovel, gently tap the sand next to one of the indents. If a razor clam is hiding there it will slowly pop out about 4 inches (10 cm) to see what's going on. Grab any razor clams you see immediately because once they figure out what's happening they'll disappear as quickly as they arrived. Once your buckets are full, it's dinnertime!

bar clams

Another very popular clam with the locals is the bar clam. Bar clams are much larger than squirt clams or quahogs, and their meat can be much tougher. These clams are harvested in greater quantities and find their way to commercial markets as breaded clam strips, in chowders and in stews. The meat in the clam is large and must be tenderized before cooking.

You'll find bar clams on shelves in local homes in the form of "bottle clams" that are cooked and bottled in brine. Often they would be kept in the cellar or cold room and pulled out to be part of a chowder, casserole or stew.

Bar clams are also perfect for clambakes on the beach. Harvesting them is a lot of fun, and it's even becoming a popular tourist adventure throughout the Island. The real fun is in the hunt. Bar clams are found on sandbars just off the shore in a few of feet of water. You need a hoe-type rake and snorkel gear and a little bit of courage for this one because you dive down to the sandbar to try to spot a large, shallow hole. You use the rake to scoop up the large clams and toss them in a bucket. Sounds easy, right? I suggest you try it and see for yourself!

champion's seafood chowder

This recipe has won four championships—three provincial and one international. It's a basic chowder recipe that's easy to make and can work for any kind of fish you have on hand. SERVES 10–12

1 lb (500 g) clams
1 lb (500 g) mussels
1 lb (500 g) lobster
1 lb (500 g) haddock (large dice)
10 cups (2.5 L) fish stock (page 244)
3 whole black peppercorns
3 sprigs fresh parsley
2 bay leaves
2 whole star anise pods
⅔ cup (160 mL) unsalted butter (softened)
2 cups (500 mL) finely diced onion
2¼ cups (560 mL) finely diced celery
1 cup (250 mL) finely diced red bell pepper
1¼ cups (310 mL) all-purpose flour
5½ cups (1.4 L) medium-diced potatoes
6 cups (1.5 L) whipping cream (scalded)
salt and white pepper

Poach all the seafood in the fish stock until partially cooked. You'll need to poach each type of seafood separately, as cooking times vary. Poach the lobster whole, then shell it and chop the lobster meat into medium dice. If you are using bar clams, chop them into medium dice as well. Set aside the poached seafood as well as the fish stock.

Make a sachet by wrapping the peppercorns, parsley, bay leaves and star anise in cheesecloth. Set aside.

In a saucepan, melt the butter and sweat the onion, celery and bell pepper. Add the flour and cook to make a blond roux. Add the fish stock gradually, whisking to work out any lumps. Bring to a boil, then reduce to a simmer. Add the herb sachet and cook for 10 minutes. Add the potatoes and continue to simmer until the potatoes are tender, about 15 minutes. Add the scalded cream and reserved seafood and stir just to combine. Simmer for an additional 5 minutes.

Remove and discard the herb sachet and season to taste with salt and white pepper. Let sit for 20 minutes, check the seasoning one last time and serve with fresh bread and great company.

=== tips ===
· *Try not to stir the chowder too much after the seafood is added or the haddock will break up and lose its texture.*
· *Any white fish works fine in this recipe. The fish can be cut into smaller pieces for a more elegant presentation, but be careful not to break up the seafood too much.*
· *For a richer chowder, finish the recipe by adding another 125 mL (½ cup) butter just before serving.*

beach clams

This recipe is almost like a travelling clambake. Barbecues are a safe, portable, easy-to-control heat source. But if you're adventurous, try barbecuing in the sand. Everything is pretty much the same except you leave your barbecue out of it—the sand pit becomes your barbecue. Try adding your favourite seafood such as lobster or crab and any other things you like with your clams. SERVES 8

enough seaweed to layer between the other ingredients (soaked in seawater)
5 lb (2.2 kg) fresh steamer clams (washed free of any sand)
2 lb (1 kg) mussels (beards removed)
2 medium onions (quartered)
2 bulbs garlic (outer skin removed)
one 3-inch (8 cm) piece ginger
8 medium potatoes (medium dice)
8 ears corn (husked, washed)
12 jumbo hotdogs (or your favourite sausage)
6 bottles of your favourite local beer
2 lb (1 kg) unsalted butter (melted)
lemon wedges, for serving

Assemble a small charcoal barbecue and start the coals burning. Let them burn for about 15 minutes then rake them to distribute them evenly. Cover the bottom of a large roasting pan with seaweed, making a layer about 2 inches (5 cm) thick. On top of this arrange the clams and mussels. Put in the onions, garlic and ginger, and then cover with a 2-inch (5 cm) layer of seaweed. Load on the potatoes, corn and hotdogs or sausages. Pour half the beer over everything and cover with a clean, damp potato sack (or lid). Place this on the barbecue and begin steaming.

Once the steam starts, let everything cook for 1 hour. Add some more beer if steam is escaping and add more charcoal if the fire degrades.

Serve family-style (that is, letting everyone help themselves), with melted butter and lemon.

One of my favourite things is an old-fashioned clambake. They bring back memories of my childhood, when we used to pack up our little boat and head out on our annual camping trip along the St. Lawrence River in Quebec. We would arrive onshore mid-afternoon, and my stepfather, Roger, would set up camp while we kids went exploring. He would give us a bucket and tell us to bring back anything edible we could find, and we'd gather snails, mussels and clams along the shore. When we came back he would have a big pot on the camp stove or a hole dug in the sand with charcoal. We would cook the clams with whatever meat and vegetables we had brought for dinner, then we'd go off on another adventure. This experience is much like the traditional clambake you will find on Prince Edward Island. Recently I was on the beach in front of my restaurant digging a hole and filling it full of charcoal. We gathered our sausages, lobster, corn, potatoes, mussels and clams and steamed everything in the sand. This is a traditional Island feast and a true expression of Island flavours.

Clam Diggers Restaurant in Georgetown sells thousands of orders of clams every season and has the reputation of having the "best clams around." The secret is in the breading and how they are handled. Each clam is pressure-shucked, and the thick skin on the tongue is removed. Every clam is breaded by hand and placed in the fryer in a particular way to ensure even cooking and proper shape. No clams are prepared ahead of time because the results would not be the same. The clams are fresh and made to order every time. The trick is to have a foolproof system. We start with a roll in flavoured pre-dust to help everything stick the way it should. Next we dip the clams in a special batter like a wash to bind the crumbs to the clam and keep the moisture in. Finally, we roll them in the Clam Diggers top-secret crumbs before popping them into the fryer. We serve them with our chunky pickle mayonnaise and lemon wedges.

When you sit on the deck at Clam Diggers you overlook three rivers: Montague River, Brudenell River and Cardigan River. During low tide, locals dig clams on the beach right in front of the restaurant, and at the end of the day the clam boats are moored in the sunset for the night. It is truly one of my favourite places on earth to spend time.

digger fried clams with chunky dill pickle mayonnaise

This is a pretty close adaptation of the fried clam recipe we use at Clam Diggers. It's almost foolproof!
SERVES 8

DILL PICKLE MAYONNAISE
1½ cups (375 mL) mayonnaise (full-fat)
3 medium dill pickles (dried with a towel, small dice)
2 Tbsp (30 mL) Frank's RedHot Chile 'n Lime Hot Sauce (or your favourite hot sauce)
2 Tbsp (30 mL) lemon juice
salt and pepper

CLAMS
1 cup (250 mL) water
4 lb (1.8 kg) steamer clams (washed free of any sand)
2 cups (500 mL) all-purpose flour
2 tsp (10 mL) dried basil
1 Tbsp (15 mL) freshly cracked black pepper
1 tsp (5 mL) salt
3 eggs
3 cups (750 mL) 2% milk
4 cups (1 L) fine dried breadcrumbs

tip
The great thing about clams is that they can stand up to just about any flavour. They work with delicate flavours such as butter, tarragon and cream but can also hold their own against strong flavours like curry, Pernod and garlic.

For the mayonnaise, combine the mayonnaise and pickles. Add the hot sauce and lemon juice and mix well. Season to taste with salt and pepper. Refrigerate until ready to serve. This will keep for up to 5 days.

Place the water and clams in a pot and steam the clams for about 6 minutes, or until the meat easily pulls away from the shell. Remove the meat, making sure to remove the tough outer skin from the tongue. Pat dry and set aside.

To make a pre-dust, combine the flour, basil, pepper and salt and mix well. Put this pre-dust on a plate and set aside.

Make an egg wash by whisking together the eggs and milk in a small stainless steel bowl. Set this aside.

Roll each clam in pre-dust, dip in the egg wash to coat, then roll in the breadcrumbs and lay on paper towel.

Preheat a deep fryer filled with oil to 375°F (190°C). If you don't have a deep fryer, you can use a large saucepan of oil, but you need to be very careful if you use this method—the oil shouldn't be more than halfway up the pot, and submerge the clams slowly into the pot.

Fry the breaded clams in batches until golden brown, about 1 minute. Remove the clams from the fryer and place them on paper towel to drain off any excess oil.

Serve with the mayonnaise and lemon wedges.

island steamers with fennel, tomato and lime

Although fried clams are still the most popular way to serve clams in restaurants, clams are finding their way onto menus in other creative ways. Of course, clam chowder often takes centre stage, but steamed clams, baked clams and clams served in pasta are becoming very popular as well.

Steaming or stewing can be a healthier choice without sacrificing any of the flavour. We sometimes serve this version at Clam Diggers. It offers bold flavour and is easy to prepare. In fact it can be prepped ahead and left waiting in the pot, so when your guests arrive, you can spend time with them instead of hovering over the stove. SERVES 8

4 lb (1.8 kg) fresh steamer clams
  (washed free of any sand)
1 cup (250 mL) small-diced fennel
1 cup (250 mL) small-diced tomato
  (skin removed)
1 Tbsp (15 mL) yellow curry paste
2 Tbsp (30 mL) unsalted butter
½ cup (125 mL) coconut milk
½ cup (125 mL) whipping cream
¼ cup (60 mL) lime juice
salt and pepper

Sauté the fresh clams, fennel, tomato and curry in the butter for 1 minute. Add the coconut milk, cream and lime juice and bring to a boil. Cover, then let simmer for about 8 minutes over medium heat or until the clams are opened and the meat can be easily pulled away from the shell.

Taste the broth and adjust the seasoning with salt if necessary. Transfer the clams to a large bowl or casserole dish. Pour the remaining broth over the clams and sprinkle with cracked pepper.

Serve with crusty bread and lime wedges.

tip

As a rule you can substitute clams for mussels in most recipes (and vice versa).

oysters Oyster Fricassee with Wilted Spinach and Chive and Caper Relish *p. 67*

PEI Oysters Five Ways *p. 69*

a day with the johnnys

Fresh, briny, crisp! Prince Edward Island oysters are yet another jewel in PEI's seafood crown. Some of the most succulent oysters in the world are grown and harvested in the waters surrounding PEI. The world-famous Malpeque oyster has spurred a major oyster aquaculture industry on PEI, to the point where each growing region produces its own particular flavour. Other popular varieties of oysters are Raspberry Points and Colville Bays.

There are two Johnnys on PEI who take their oyster business very seriously: oyster farmer (and lobster fisher) Johnny Flynn of Souris's Colville Bay Oysters, and John Bil, a world champion oyster shucker and restaurateur, who shares his passion for Prince Edward Island oysters with anyone who dares slurp one of these tasty morsels.

After spending an evening wading along the shoreline of Colville Bay with Johnny Flynn, I was truly enlightened on the topic of the regional idiosyncrasies that make Colville Bay oysters unique. Johnny first told me about the terroir, the saltwater flats that are washed daily with fresh water from the Souris River. Speaking as a chef, I think that is where the "crisp" comes in. The briny liquor of the oyster has a freshness from the river water to balance the saltiness of the ocean. Johnny's oysters also have a unique look about them thanks to the algae-rich tinge of green that paints the edges of the white shell. The algae thrive in the warm waters of the flats during low tide when the sun can raise the temperature by a degree or two. If you were to take Colville Bay oysters (from eastern PEI) and Raspberry Point oysters (from the north shore Cavendish area) and set them down side by side, you would see the difference in their shell colour and taste their different flavours. The Raspberry Points have an obviously higher salinity in the oyster liquor, another difference that can reveal their terroir. It's amazing how much the oysters are affected by their specific geography.

The best way to find out about oysters is to take the time to talk to the oyster farmers who troll these waters 10 months of the year. They're totally tuned in to any changes in the water, the breeding ground for this vibrant PEI aquaculture industry. Johnny uses the French rack system for growing spat (really small oysters). Baby oysters are protected by a black mesh bag until they're big enough to be spread in specific beds. Their growth is tracked by age; it takes an oyster four to five years to reach a saleable size.

Johnny told us how Quebec oyster connoisseurs prefer a larger oyster than those oyster lovers on the east coast. He does grow some oysters larger for his special customers, but for Johnny it's all about quality over size.

He doesn't want the business to grow too large. It's plain to see that he just loves doing what he's doing. He was out this evening with his daughter Sarah, who is the oyster gal in the family—she loves it as much as Johnny does. It is reassuring to know that the next generation will be just as passionate about oysters. With Johnny running his business with his brother Leo, this oyster business is a real family affair.

John Bil is another PEI oyster ambassador. He's also a world champion oyster shucker, and he's fast, let me tell you. But fast isn't enough—you have to be efficient, too. John feels the oyster to find its most vulnerable point of entry, then skilfully sweeps his blade through the muscle connected to the shell, being careful not to disturb the rest of the oyster. He wants every oyster to be perfect.

I recently spent a weekend hanging out with John at an industry trade show where we were both representing Prince Edward Island. John is quick-tongued and can talk to anyone—to willing participants in his oyster experience as well as to those who are more hesitant. And with the latter, John has a tenacity that wears down their fears; a good portion end up doing as they are told, chewing the oyster then sending it down the hatch.

A number of condiments are standard artillery for an oyster bar. When we serve oysters, we usually have people start with a lemon wedge (of course), then move on to hot sauce (a few varieties and heat levels), fresh ground pepper, mignonette and seafood sauce. (My preference is just a squeeze of lemon with a splash of hot sauce . . . wow!)

It's people like John, who are just as passionate about these oysters as the farmer that cultivated them, who keep this industry alive.

colville bay
oysters
in the raw,
on the shell

As a chef on PEI, I regard oysters as one of those local ingredients that are a fantastic conversation piece. You can always get someone talking over this tasty bivalve. Something we chefs have come to know and accept, though, is that if you've tried them, you either love them or you hate them. If you love them, welcome aboard! Served chilled on ice with a variety of sauces and condiments, or served hot (steamed, gratinéed or baked)—either way, they are delicious. Or why not keep it simple? The crisp, clean brininess of a freshly shucked oyster is a tasty experience.

When it comes to Colville Bay oysters, I'd say these tasty little gems are best served well chilled, and shucked outside on a deck, on the wharf or on the shore. While I was checking out Johnny Flynn's location, we washed more than a few down with a couple of cold beers. We were well armed with a lemon cut in half to squeeze over the oysters and a bottle of my favourite hot sauce.

*Approximately 6 million pounds (2.7 million kg)
of oysters are harvested on Prince Edward Island every year.
Most of the harvest is exported to a selection
of major North American cities.*

oyster fricassee with wilted spinach and chive and caper relish

This is a fantastic yet simple oyster dish with a big, round flavour and nice presentation. The oysters are poached in their own liquid (or "liquor"), which then becomes the sauce. This is a great dish to impress your significant other—or a potential significant other! The relish is at its best if you prepare it the day before and let the flavours blend. SERVES 4

CHIVE AND CAPER RELISH
¼ cup (60 mL) chopped capers
2 Tbsp (30 mL) red onion, minced
juice and zest of ½ lemon
¼ cup (60 mL) chopped chives
2 Tbsp (30 mL) chopped fresh dill
1 Tbsp (15 mL) black truffle oil
1 Tbsp (15 mL) white balsamic vinegar
salt and pepper

FRICASSEE
2 Tbsp (30 mL) unsalted butter
2 Tbsp (30 mL) minced green onion
1 tsp (5 mL) minced garlic
12 Colville Bay oysters (shucked
  and liquor reserved)
¼ cup (60 mL) vermouth
½ cup (125 mL) crème fraîche
  (or full-fat sour cream)

salt and pepper
½ cup (125 mL) chopped chives
12 slices baguette

SPINACH
2 cups (500 mL) baby spinach
1 Tbsp (15 mL) vermouth
salt and pepper

For the relish, combine all the relish ingredients in a medium-sized bowl. Refrigerate for 2 to 3 days, until needed.

For the fricassee, in a skillet on medium heat place the butter, green onion and garlic. Cook slightly until tender. Add the oysters, sauté slightly and deglaze with the vermouth and reserved oyster liquor. Add the crème fraîche, remove from the heat and season to taste with salt and pepper. Add the chopped chives, keep warm and reserve.

For the spinach, in a skillet on medium heat, add the spinach and vermouth. Wilt the spinach slightly, then season to taste with salt and pepper.

Serve the oysters on slices of fresh baguette, layered as follows: slice of bread, layer of spinach, oyster and sauce, topped with some relish.

PEI oysters five ways

"Some like 'em hot and some like 'em cold." Here are five ways to serve our famous oysters, a range of preparations that really shows the versatility of the oyster. I guess that's what we chefs appreciate about it. As the Island's oyster industry continues to evolve, chefs will continue dreaming up new and exciting preparations that highlight this little gem. Serve up oyster dishes with a nice glass of Sauvignon Blanc.

herb and potato–crusted oysters

This recipe is delicious and is a great way to introduce oysters to those who may shy away from eating them. It takes some people a few steps before they can graduate to the chilled oyster in the raw! SERVES 4

1 cup (250 mL) instant mashed potato flakes
½ cup (125 mL) chopped assorted fresh
    herbs (tarragon, thyme, basil, chives)
salt and pepper
12 live oysters, shucked
2 Tbsp (30 mL) unsalted butter (softened)
sour cream as needed (full-fat gives the best
    results in this recipe)

In a small bowl, combine the mashed potato flakes, herbs and salt and pepper to taste. Take a freshly shucked oyster, place it in the bowl and cover liberally with the flake mixture. Repeat for the remaining oysters.

Place a small skillet over high heat and add the butter. Quickly add the crusted oysters and brown until golden all around. Serve with a dollop of sour cream and fresh cracked pepper.

smoked and poked

You'll need a stovetop smoker for this one. SERVES 4

12 live oysters (shucked)
3 Tbsp (45 mL) salted butter

On a small stovetop smoker (see tip below) place the shucked oysters on the screen. Cover the oysters and put the heat on high.

When the smoke starts to slowly billow, let the smoker sit for 2 minutes, reducing the heat to low.

Remove the oysters from the smoker screen. In a small skillet, add the butter. Add the oysters to the hot pan, quickly sear on one side and then flip to sear the second side. Spear with a toothpick to remove from the pan and serve immediately.

=== ❦ tip ❦ ===

You can assemble a makeshift hot smoker on your stovetop. I would recommend that you open a window or turn on your hood fan before trying this. You are going to need two old skillets that you can keep for this purpose and a square piece of metal screen that is just as large as the skillets. Sprinkle the bottom of the bottom pan with water-dampened wood chips—find apple wood, maple, mesquite and hickory in specialty stores, or ask a local woodworker to save some for you. Place the screen on top of one skillet and cover with the other. It's a bit crude, but it does the job. Turn the flame on low, and let the chips heat up. You will see the smoke slowly billowing out between the pans. Be careful to control the amount of heat.

continued . . .

PEI OYSTERS FIVE WAYS *continued*

mignonette

This is a classic French preparation. SERVES 4

¼ cup (60 mL) red wine vinegar
2 Tbsp (30 mL) minced red onion
salt and pepper
12 live oysters (shucked just before using)

Combine the vinegar, onion, and salt and pepper to taste. Spoon over a freshly shucked oyster.

caesar ice

A twist on the classic east coast favourite. SERVES 4

¼ cup (60 mL) vodka
½ cup (125 mL) Clamato juice
hot sauce
pepper
2 drops Worcestershire sauce
12 live oysters (shucked just before using)

Combine all the ingredients, except the oysters, in a metal bowl. Place in the freezer and let set, 2 hours. When frozen, scrape with a spoon and serve atop a freshly shucked oyster.

oyster martini

A real twist on the shaken not stirred; this is shucked then stirred! SERVES 1

1 live oyster (shucked)
½ fl oz (15 mL) vodka or gin
splash vermouth
splash fresh lemon juice
salt and pepper
1 black or green olive

In a shot glass, place the freshly shucked oyster. Top with vodka or gin and a splash of vermouth. Add the lemon juice, salt and pepper and olive. Stir and enjoy!

lobsters

a day on the water

Once known as "poor man's food" here on Prince Edward Island, our lobster is now a local delicacy like no other. Setting Day marks the opening of the spring fishery, a day that all lobster lovers wait for anxiously to indulge in the first feed of the season. Mother's Day falls soon after Setting Day, and it is a common family tradition to treat Mom to a feed of these not-so-pretty but delicious little creatures. Whether it is on a picnic table in the backyard or at one of PEI's famous "church lobster suppers," the arrival of lobster season has woven its way tightly into the culinary fabric of the Island.

In my opinion lobsters have to be one of the tastiest and most special creatures in the ocean. Prince Edward Island has a plentiful catch that runs from May to June on the north side of the Island and from August to September on the south. These creatures, with their big bulging eyes, live on the floor of the ocean where they scavenge for food and travel with the tides in some of the cleanest waters in the world.

We wouldn't have access to these wonderful creatures if it weren't for our fishers, though. A typical day on the water first has them leaving their wharves well before sunrise. They sail in a 40- to 50-foot (12- to 15-metre) boat, usually equipped with a cabin that contains a stove, fridge and washroom, plus a very sophisticated navigation system. The captain will be accompanied by one or two mates. They sail for 30 minutes to 1 hour (sometimes longer) offshore to where they have previously scattered their rope-bound traps that have been marked with a uniquely painted and numbered buoy. Three hundred traps set in bunches of five or six are pulled (bunch by bunch) from the cool, clean Atlantic waters with the help of a hydraulic winch. One by one each trap is emptied, topped up with bait and plunged back into the water to sit on the rocky bottom for another 24 hours. Personally, I check that the weather is going to be good with little wind before I venture out on the water. The fishers, though, usually go out no matter what, and some days can be pretty rough at sea. But some days are just *too* rough and windy, and they will leave their traps for the next day. I have driven along the shore and seen the huge whitecaps bobbing the boats up and down and side to side. Sometimes the water in early spring can make you cold just by looking at it, but day after day the fishers get in their boats and sail to their traps in hopes of another great catch.

cooking lobsters

Fishers usually recommend that lobsters always be cooked in a very large pot of boiling seawater. A homemade saltwater brine with 3 percent salt content is a good substitute (about 11 oz/300 g salt for every 9 quarts/10 L of water). Remove the rubber claw bands, then plunge the lobster into the boiling water and cook according to the weight of the lobster. You should allow 12 minutes for a 1-pound (500 g) lobster to cook, increasing cooking time by 1 minute for every additional ¼ pound (125 g) of lobster. This means, for example, that a 1½-pound (750 g) lobster should be cooked for 14 minutes.

We have a few recipes using lobster meat: lobster cakes, bouillabaisse, even mashed potatoes (page 190). Another great way to enjoy lobster is in a sandwich. Here's a simple recipe:

Mix together 2 cups (500 mL) chopped cooked lobster meat, ½ cup (125 mL) mayonnaise, ¼ cup (60 mL) diced celery and 2 Tbsp (30 mL) chopped fresh herbs (like parsley, tarragon and/or dill). Season to taste with salt and pepper. Serve on fresh bread (homemade would be perfect!), with crisp lettuce. (This filling is enough for 4 sandwiches.)

rustico-style lobster supper

I am often asked, "Where should I go to enjoy a good lobster dinner?" and I always give the same answer. Many restaurants on Prince Edward Island offer the diner an unforgettable lobster experience. Take your pick of these restaurants, or try one of the many church lobster suppers that are offered across the Island. But in my opinion, the best way to enjoy lobster is to sit outside on a picnic table overlooking the water. That's how it's done here on the Island. We locals go down to the wharf and purchase directly from the fishers. You can't get any fresher than that.

To enjoy lobster in the summer outside and near the water, you will need to assemble a few things, including, of course, some cold beverages of your choice. Then you can simply sit down and enjoy the best lobster experience of your life.

Cooked 1 lb (500 g) lobsters (according to appetites—we recommend a minimum of 1 lobster per person)
Drawn butter
Roasted Red Pepper Potato Salad (page 193)
Coleslaw (page 154)
Fresh bread
Butter
Lobster bibs
Lobster picks
Lobster crackers
Lots of napkins

The female lobsters are sometimes preferred because they hold the succulent red roe or eggs that the true lobster lover hopes to find. Some consumers will actually request a female lobster when ordering in a restaurant or fish market. You can tell the sex of a lobster by uncurling and looking at its tail. The female's is slightly bowed in the middle whereas the male's is straight and narrow. You can also turn the lobster upside down and feel the set of swimmerets that are closest to the body on the underside of the lobster. The male ones are firm whereas the female ones are soft and pliable.

lobster bouillabaisse

This lobster recipe has quite a bit of history attached to it. In France, fishers would return to port with the day's catch and sell it to the locals. If they had any fish left they would make large fish stews for their own families. This stew was called bouillabaisse. *My version uses only lobster, but you can use any type of seafood that you wish.* SERVES 4

four 1 lb (500 g) lobsters
1 Tbsp (15 mL) olive oil
2 Tbsp (30 mL) minced green onion
1 Tbsp (15 mL) minced garlic
¼ cup (60 mL) dry white wine
3 cups (750 mL) lobster stock (page 245)
   (made with shells from lobsters above)
3 cups (750 mL) fish stock (page 244)
2 cups (500 mL) cut vegetables of your choice
   (carrots, celery, fennel, white turnip and
   new potatoes work great)
½ cup (125 mL) leek julienne
pinch Spanish saffron
salt and pepper
1 Tbsp (15 mL) chopped fresh parsley

Cook the lobsters in a large pot of boiling salted water for 12 minutes. Remove from the pot, allow to cool, then shell, keeping the shells to make the stock.

In a large pot, heat the olive oil over medium heat and sauté the shallots and garlic for 2 to 3 minutes. Add the white wine and reduce by half. Add the lobster stock, fish stock, vegetables (including the leek) and saffron. Bring this to a boil, then reduce to a gentle simmer and cook until the vegetables are tender, 15 to 20 minutes. Add the reserved lobster and season to taste with salt and pepper. Warm through the lobster, being careful not to overcook it. Check the seasoning and adjust if necessary. Top with fresh chopped parsley and serve with crusty French bread on the side.

=== tip ===

Remove the rubber bands from the lobster's claws before cooking. The bands will discolour the shell and affect the taste of the meat.

Lobsters moult (that is, shed their outer shell) usually once a year when the waters warm up and food is plentiful. The lobster uses its protein and energy reserves to begin growing a new shell underneath its current one. It squeezes out of the old shell and then takes in water so that it starts to swell. This swelling makes the new shell bigger. The lobster then eats the old shell, which is full of calcium and very nutritious.

saffron butter–poached lobster

In a chef's world, lobster is one of the best things you can offer a guest. Boiling and steaming are the most common ways to cook this crustacean. These do produce a delicious meal, but chefs are always pushing the envelope! Grilling, broiling, sautéing and butter-poaching lobster are a few different approaches you might want to explore.

This recipe has long been a favourite of mine. It is a bit of work because you must partially boil the lobster, shell it and then poach it in butter. But of course it's well worth the effort. SERVES 4

1 medium red onion (small dice)
1 clove garlic (minced)
3 Tbsp (45 mL) olive oil
2 pinches saffron
¼ cup (60 mL) dry white wine
1 cup (250 mL) fish stock (page 244)
1 lb (500 g) unsalted butter
    (cold, small cubes)
salt
four 1 lb (500 g) fresh lobsters

Over medium heat, sauté the onion and garlic in the olive oil until translucent, 2 to 3 minutes. Add the saffron, stir and deglaze the pan with the white wine. Add the fish stock and bring to a simmer. Allow to cool slightly, then transfer to a blender and purée until smooth. Strain through a fine-mesh sieve. Return the puréed liquid to the pot and, using minimal heat, begin adding the cubes of butter while whisking, to create an emulsion. Reserve and keep warm.

Bring a large pot—large enough to hold all 4 lobsters at one time—of water to boil, adding salt to taste. Place the lobsters in the boiling water and cook for 5 minutes. Begin timing once the water has returned to a boil. Remove the claws from the lobster, let cool and place the remainder of the lobster back into the boiling water for an additional 5 minutes. Remove the lobster from the pot. Remove the meat from shells, keeping the tails and claws intact. This is an art in itself. The tail can be removed from the shell with a fork quite easily, but the claws require a bit more finesse. It is best to remove the claws while they are still hot.

To serve, warm the poaching liquid gently, just until you see bubbles gradually breaking the surface (about 175°F/80°C). Place the tail and claw meat in the poaching liquid and cook for 4 to 5 minutes to warm through. Serve the poaching liquid as the sauce.

lobster and potato cakes

Many people love fish cakes. Here is my favourite recipe for lobster cakes. It is very simple and can be made well in advance. SERVES 4

4 medium Yukon Gold potatoes (cooked, mashed, chilled)
1 cup (250 mL) coarsely chopped lobster meat (claws and knuckles, chilled)
½ cup (125 mL) grated cheddar (chilled)
¼ cup (60 mL) sour cream (chilled)
2 slices bacon (cooked, crumbled, chilled)
3 Tbsp (45 mL) chopped fresh parsley, chives, dill and/or tarragon
salt and pepper
coarse breadcrumbs (Japanese panko preferred) (more for coating)

COATING
¼ cup (60 mL) all-purpose flour (seasoned with a pinch of salt and pepper)
½ cup (125 mL) egg wash (page 251)
½ cup (125 mL) coarse breadcrumbs (Japanese panko preferred)
1 Tbsp (15 mL) unsalted butter (softened)

Make sure that all the cake ingredients are thoroughly chilled before you begin.

For the cakes, gently mix the potatoes, lobster, cheese, sour cream, bacon and herbs (overmixing will cause the starch in the potatoes to become gluey). Season to taste with salt and pepper.

Form the mixture into 8 evenly sized cakes. Refrigerate until they are cool enough to easily hold their shape, about 1 hour. If the mixture is too wet, add a few breadcrumbs to absorb some of the moisture.

Preheat the oven to 350°F (180°C). Grease a baking sheet.

Dredge the lobster cakes in the seasoned flour, dip in the egg wash, coat evenly with breadcrumbs, dip again in the egg wash and finally coat again with the breadcrumbs.

Preheat a skillet to medium heat, melt the butter and gently sauté the cakes until golden on both sides, 2 to 3 minutes per side. Transfer to the prepared baking sheet, place in the oven and cook for 6 to 8 minutes. (If you have an ovenproof skillet you can use this for both cooking stages.)

lobster facts

- A good day's catch, according to some fishers, is 1½ to 2 lb (750 g to 1 kg) of lobster per trap.
- Market lobsters weigh in at 1 lb (500 g) or more; canner lobsters weigh in at 1 lb (500 g) or less.
- Fishers are only permitted 300 traps each.
- The carapace or body of the lobster must be at least 2¹³⁄₁₆ inches (71 mm) in length when measured from the eye to the back centre of the body. If too small, it must be returned to the ocean.

- There cannot be any visible eggs on the underside of a female's tail. If there are, it must be returned to the ocean.
- PEI fishers bring in over 20 million pounds (over 9 million kg) of lobster every year.
- Roe is the red substance found in the tail of a cooked female lobster.
- Tomalley is the liver of the lobster. It is greenish and pretty tasty!

tuna

giants from the deep

The tuna fishery is one of the most exciting fisheries on Prince Edward Island. These mammoth fish,
some weighing in excess of 1,100 lb (over 500 kg),
are certainly a handful for the fisher who finds one
on the end of his or her line. That's a lot of tuna
steaks! And from a chef's perspective, blue fin tuna
is a true delicacy. In fact, it is such a delicacy that
buyers from fish markets in Japan lie in wait on
the wharves of North Lake, Naufrage, Rustico and
Tignish for the daily catch.

Prince Edward Island has long been a destination for sport anglers looking for a challenge. Their
reward is the Atlantic blue fin tuna. For many years,
PEI was known as the blue fin tuna capital of the
world. It was chaos when the fish started to run,
chasing the herring schools on the Gulf Stream.
Sport fishers quickly came in search of the thrill of a
lifetime, the prospect of hooking one of these giants
on the end of their line.

Unfortunately, for several years, tuna stocks
were in decline, and only a few fish were caught in
the waters around PEI, but in the late 1990s there
was a resurgence of blue fin tuna, and, in 2000,
they were so plentiful that PEI reclaimed its title.
This was an exciting time to be a chef on Prince
Edward Island.

Even the photo shoot for this book reflected the reality of being a chef on PEI. We had put the call out to the local fishers in Rustico (you know who you are!) that we needed a tuna, and we got a call on a Monday afternoon. But not any old Monday.

This was opening day of the tuna fishery in August. (There's another one that takes place in late September/early October.) There was a tuna on its way to the wharf. Lee Gallant had landed the first fish of the season, and the crew would be at the wharf at 5 p.m. Cell phones begin to chime as everyone called all the necessary people with the news to get things ready to roll. We all dropped what we were doing and headed out to Rustico. Even in all the excitement I found myself thinking how much I loved this place. Small and rural and with all the necessities—a bank, a hardware store, a grocery store and even a liquor store. We parked our cars at Joey's place and jumped into a speedboat to make our way down the river to the wharf. We wouldn't have to deal with the crowd at the wharf that way, and we'd be able to just pull alongside Lee's boat to get the shots we wanted.

What a rush this was. Everyone's adrenaline was pumping, all of us caught up in the moment of the first tuna landing. The fish was hoisted out of the water and hung up for the crowd to admire and photograph. The captain and crew were very happy with their catch. (I imagine their heads were swirling with questions: weight, quality, price?) The fish was then weighed, cleaned and quickly packed on ice.

Luckily we landed the tail from this fish; we needed it for the photo shoot. Things just came together for us. It was an awesome rush for a seasoned chef and quite an exciting experience for the first-timers in the group. The local crowd gathered, flashes still flashing, the oohs and aahs coming from the crowd as the people eyed this fish with amazement. It really was a magnificent fish.

We headed back to town with the tail in tow, packed on ice, and the ideas started to rush into my mind. What in my kitchen was going to complement this fish to bring the final dish to its full potential? When you are a chef from Prince Edward Island and have the opportunity to showcase so many wonderful ingredients, your imagination goes into overdrive. The possibilities are endless in early August on the Garden of the Gulf.

The fishers in North Lake would call us at the restaurant when they were on their way inshore with a tuna. We would jump in our rig and make the exciting 25-minute journey to the wharf. We knew that there would be tuna on the menu that night. The only question was, what form would it take? Ceviche, seared, tartare—which one would it be?

On one occasion we had lots of fresh wild watercress that would accompany a North Lake Blue Fin Tuna duo—one quick Sesame-Seared Tuna with Wild Watercress and Soy Maple Vinaigrette, and one Chili and Lime Tartare with Fresh Cilantro from the herb garden (see page 93 for the recipes). We decided to top this dish off with a couple of well-placed black sesame crackers.

Whenever we set off to collect a tuna, we would be overcome by excitement about getting such a delicacy for nothing! The fisher would remove the head and tail from the great fish. We would get maybe a foot and half of tuna loin from the tail piece. The top prize, though, was the cheeks—the jowls of the fish. We would butcher the head right on the wharf and quickly get the fish on ice. At $15 a plate these fresh-as-you-can-get tuna appetizers are a steal. Diners in Japan would pay dearly to be so closely connected to the fish they adore.

We would then watch the buyers bid and outbid for the fish. First, the appraisers would take a core sample of the flesh to scrutinize it for firmness, clarity, colour and texture. They would set the base price, and the bidding would begin. It wasn't unheard of to have a fish in excess of 1,000 lb (450 kg) going for $40 per pound. That is a whopping price for a whopping fish. The tuna would then be cleaned, dressed and crated on ice and taken directly to Charlottetown for the first cargo flight to Japan.

We've had Japanese tourists ask for the head of the fish to use the eyeballs for fish-eye soup. Apparently this is a rare delicacy, although it's something we have yet to try.

Back to Bay Fortune we would go, making a quick stop to top up our watercress supply for that night's cold side dish. The excitement would continue to mount until we had the first plate ready. I would assemble the dish for the crew to critique. I wanted them all to *see it and taste it*. It was as though this freshly seared portion of tuna was still quivering. Served with quickly wilted watercress drizzled with the sweet and sour vinaigrette . . . wow! What a treat for the taste buds.

two quick ways with blue fin tuna

sesame-seared tuna with wild watercress and soy maple vinaigrette

Ask your local fish shop to give you tuna already butchered into cubes. SERVES 2

- 2 Tbsp (30 mL) sesame oil
- 4 oz (60 g) fresh blue fin tuna (cut in 2-inch/5 cm cubes)
- salt and pepper
- 2 handfuls wild watercress
- splash rice wine vinegar
- ¼ cup (60 mL) black and white sesame seeds
- 2 Tbsp (30 mL) maple syrup
- 2 Tbsp (30 mL) soy sauce

In a skillet, add the sesame oil and bring up to high heat. Season the tuna well and place it in the hot skillet. After 30 seconds, turn and cook it for 1 minute more. Remove the tuna from the pan and keep warm until needed. Quickly add the watercress to the hot pan. Add a splash of rice wine vinegar, then the sesame seeds, maple syrup and soy sauce. Season to taste with salt and pepper.

Cut each cube of tuna in half. It should be "medium-rare" in the centre. Drizzle the vinaigrette over the tuna and spoon around the plate. Enjoy!

chili and lime tartare with fresh cilantro

In this recipe, the acid from the lime juice "cooks" the fish. Tartare is a French term and usually describes a beef tenderloin dish. Tuna is a very meaty fish and lends itself to this fresh, citrusy preparation. SERVES 2

- 4 oz (125 g) fresh blue fin tuna
- juice and zest of 1 lime
- 2 Tbsp (30 mL) extra virgin olive oil
- 2 Tbsp (30 mL) chopped fresh cilantro
- 1 Tbsp (15 mL) minced red onion
- salt and pepper

Mince the tuna with a chef's knife and place it in a bowl. Add in the lime juice and zest, olive oil, cilantro and red onion. Season to taste with salt and pepper.

Let sit for 5 minutes. Serve with a few slices of fresh bread or sesame crackers. Enjoy!

---

tip

There are two ways to toast sesame seeds:
- *Put them in a small skillet without oil on the stovetop on high heat. Stir frequently until toasted brown.*
- *Set them on a pie plate or ovenproof skillet and put them in a 400°F (200°C) oven for 2 to 3 minutes, bringing them out to stir frequently. Either way, toasting the sesame seeds enhances the sesame flavour with a nutty intensity.*

Blue fin tuna are a protected pelagic species (living close to the ocean's surface), and fishing quotas are issued for each region by the Department of Fisheries and Oceans. Last year's landed quota in PEI was 105 tonnes. The blue fin tuna fishery is crucial for Prince Edward Island. The Japanese market pays top money for the tuna caught off our waters, and sold to restaurants for sushi and sashimi. It can be a huge payday for the captain and crew who land one of these fish. Blue fin tuna is a very lucrative fishery option for Island fishers, as long as stocks stay plentiful.

grilled curried blue fin tuna and pineapple salad with coriander yogurt dressing

This is a great summer salad. I love Indian-inspired food, and even my three-year-old loves this dish. The barbecue marinade for the tuna works well with the yogurt dressing to cool things down in the heat of the summer. SERVES 4

MARINADE

½ cup (125 mL) red pepper jelly
¼ cup (60 mL) prepared Italian dressing
3 Tbsp (45 mL) curry paste (strength according to taste)
2 Tbsp (30 mL) yellow mustard

TUNA

four 4 oz (125 g) fresh blue fin tuna steaks

DRESSING

¾ cup (190 mL) Balkan-style yogurt
¼ cup (60 mL) chopped fresh coriander
¼ cup (60 mL) chopped fresh mint
½ cup (125 mL) canola oil
¼ cup (60 mL) white wine vinegar
2 Tbsp (30 mL) minced red onion
2 Tbsp (30 mL) honey
1 Tbsp (15 mL) minced fresh ginger

SALAD

four ½-inch (1 cm) slices golden pineapple
chipotle Tabasco sauce
3 cups (750 mL) mixed salad greens
20 grape or cherry tomatoes (halved)
½ English cucumber (unpeeled, thinly sliced into rounds)
½ cup (125 mL) combination of thinly sliced red, green and yellow bell peppers

¼ cup (60 mL) thinly sliced red onion
¼ cup (60 mL) sliced almonds
8 strawberries
4 sprigs fresh cilantro

For the marinade, combine all 4 ingredients in a bowl and whisk them together. Transfer the marinade to a medium-sized Ziploc bag and add the 4 tuna steaks. Refrigerate for at least 2 hours, or overnight.

For the dressing, combine all the ingredients in a blender and blend well. Refrigerate until needed. This keeps well for 1 week if stored in an airtight container.

Preheat the grill to medium-high.

Grill the tuna until it is cooked to your preference. If you like it more on the rare side, allow 1 to 2 minutes per side depending on the thickness; if you like it more well done, allow 3 to 4 minutes per side. Turn the fish only once. Brush with some of the marinade as you are grilling.

For the salad, grill the pineapple, brushing it with the chipotle Tabasco sauce as you go. Flip it over and reapply some Tabasco. Take each slice of grilled pineapple and cut it into quarters.

Place the mixed salad greens in a bowl. Add the tomatoes, cucumber, bell peppers, onion and almonds. Add an ample amount of dressing and toss.

Slice the grilled tuna, place it on top of the salad and top with the pineapple, strawberries and fresh cilantro.

tuna burger with maple mayonnaise and spicy apple slaw

This is a great fish sandwich. The Asian-inspired crispy apple slaw and the sweetness of the maple mayo complement the tuna nicely, playing off its "beefy" flavour. For the tuna, you can use blue fin if it's available, but yellow fin or albacore would be acceptable substitutions. They are smaller species of tuna and more readily available from your local fish market.

SERVES 4

SLAW

1 apple (sliced into thin strips)
1 green onion (thinly sliced)
1 cup (250 mL) thinly sliced cabbage
¼ cup (60 mL) capers (drained)
¼ cup (60 mL) cider vinegar
2 Tbsp (30 mL) black sesame seeds
2 Tbsp (30 mL) sunflower oil
pinch Chinese five-spice powder
salt and pepper

MAPLE MAYONNAISE

1 cup (250 mL) mayonnaise
2 Tbsp (30 mL) maple syrup
1 Tbsp (15 mL) grainy mustard
salt and pepper

BURGERS

2 Tbsp (30 mL) olive oil
four 4 oz (125 g) fresh tuna steaks
salt and pepper
4 fresh kaisers (cut in half)
lettuce

For the slaw, combine all the ingredients in a bowl and reserve.

For the maple mayonnaise, combine all the mayonnaise ingredients in a small bowl. Mix well and refrigerate.

For the burgers, in a skillet, add the olive oil and bring up to high heat. Season the tuna steaks well and place them in the hot skillet. After 30 seconds, turn and cook for 1 minute longer.

Assemble the burger by spreading a generous tablespoonful (15 mL +) of maple mayonnaise on the bottom half of a bun. Add a leaf or two of lettuce, then place the tuna on top and finish off with a tablespoonful or two (15 to 30 mL) of the slaw. Cap with the top half of the bun and enjoy.

= ᎒ tip ᎒ =

This tuna burger is almost as beefy as a hamburger. The oil-rich flesh is best served medium-rare, as it dries out when overcooked.

grilled north lake tuna niçoise

Niçoise is a classic cooking term that means "in the style of Nice." This means that it combines some of the classic flavours from this region of France. I like it because it shows off some of the key garden ingredients available in August on Prince Edward Island. Baby potatoes, green beans and tomatoes are all at their peak. Throw in black olives, artichokes, hard-boiled eggs and red onion, and you have a yummy salad that will surely impress. SERVES 4

BALSAMIC GLAZE
1 cup (250 mL) balsamic vinegar
¼ cup (60 mL) honey

SALAD
four 8 oz (250 g) fresh blue fin tuna fillets
½ cup (120 mL) extra virgin olive oil, divided
2 Tbsp (30 mL) chopped fresh parsley
2 Tbsp (30 mL) chopped fresh tarragon
sea salt (crushed)
cracked black pepper
1 lb (500 g) baby potatoes (blanched and quartered)
5 oz (150 g) green beans (trimmed)
1 cup (250 mL) sliced red onion
⅓ cup (80 mL) pitted black olives (kalamata or your favourite)
pinch minced garlic
1 Tbsp (15 mL) Pommery mustard (see page 23)
1 cup (250 mL) halved cherry tomatoes
1 cup (250 mL) artichoke hearts

For the glaze, in a small heavy-bottomed saucepan, combine the balsamic vinegar and the honey over high heat. Reduce the heat to medium until the mixture becomes syrupy, about 10 minutes. Remove from the pan to cool and transfer to a jar. This glaze keeps well in the refrigerator for a couple of weeks.

Preheat a charboiler or barbecue.

For the salad, rub the tuna fillets with ¼ cup (60 mL) of the olive oil (reserve the leftover oil for the vegetables) and half the chopped herbs. Season to taste with sea salt and cracked black pepper. Place on the charboiler or barbecue and cook to the desired level of doneness.

While the tuna is cooking, heat a large skillet on medium-high heat. Add the remaining ¼ cup (60 mL) of the olive oil. Add the baby potatoes and green beans and cook for 4 minutes. Add the sliced red onion, olives and garlic, and sauté until the potatoes are hot and the beans are tender. Be careful not to burn the garlic, as it will leave a bitter taste in the salad. Add the mustard, tomatoes, artichoke hearts and salt and pepper to taste. Toss just until the artichokes are warm, 2 to 3 minutes. Add the remaining chopped herbs and toss gently. Arrange equal amounts on 4 plates and place a grilled tuna fillet on top of each serving.

Lightly drizzle each plate with the balsamic glaze to taste.

apples

"A" is for apple

Apples have always been one of those crops that were grown on a farm to help the farm be self-sustaining. Every farm had a few apple trees, regardless of the type of farm. Traditionally, Cortlands, Macs and the odd russet tree kept the farm family's cellar stocked with apples for a cold winter. Nowadays, small commercial orchards scattered all over the Island give us chefs bushels of apples to use in the fall. Whether you are in Arlington Orchards in the west, at Ricky MacPhee's orchard in Woodville Mills in the east or in one of the many places in between like Marc Brunet's Olde Towne Orchard in Fredericton, you'll see evidence that the apple-growing tradition here on the Island continues to thrive.

How many of you have heard your doctor say to have an apple a day? Well, okay, maybe it wasn't your doctor exactly, but all I can say is that whoever said it is right. Apples contain vitamins A, B6, C, E and K, beta carotene, calcium, iron, magnesium, phosphorus, potassium and many other top-notch nutrients. But apples are not only nutritious; they're also very tasty, and they come in many exciting varieties.

Prince Edward Island produces approximately 450,000 pounds (over 200,000 kg) of apples every year. Most of the orchards in PEI have a u-pick option. Whole families come to make a complete day of picking apples, having lunch, taking a wagon ride with the farmer or just enjoying a day out of the house. It's a real cultural experience, and it's a great way to teach your children to love fresh fruit.

Apples have been around forever, but the art of hybridizing apples—where the orchard master crosses one tree with another—only began in the early 1800s. This is not genetic modification but rather just a blending of two varieties of fruit in hopes of finding a new apple that contains the best characteristics of the varieties being crossed. John McIntosh grafted what is probably one of the better-known varieties, the McIntosh, on his farm in Dundas, Ontario, in 1811. In the 1970s a new variety of apple was grafted in the United States. Named the Honeycrisp, it became commercially available in the 1990s. It has to be the best apple in the world for eating raw by itself. I'd be surprised if you disagreed. My grandmother introduced me to this apple at a time when it could only be found in remote farmers' markets. Today Honeycrisps can be found in many places, including the Olde Towne Orchard, which is one of two orchards on PEI that has this variety.

Olde Towne Orchard boasts five varieties of apples grown on 600 dwarf trees that are perfectly aligned on a 10-acre parcel of land on the heritage road called Warburton. The orchard, located just off the main highway in Fredericton, PEI, is owned and operated by Marc Brunet, a very passionate man who lives for good food, wine and conversation. He purchased the orchard in 2008 and quickly mastered the art of growing apples. You can pick your own apples or purchase those hand-picked by the hired help (usually Marc's two daughters, Camille and Florence, and his lovely wife, Josée).

I have spent some time with Marc in the orchard, and I can tell you that the work not only is physically demanding, with a lot of stretching, bending and lifting necessary during the harvest season, and time consuming, but also requires a lot of skill. Marc starts his year in late winter by inspecting the trees to locate and remove any limbs that might have been damaged by the Island's cold, snowy winters.

He will then begin to prune branches to make room for the apples to grow and to have maximum access to sunlight. Now, cutting off a few limbs doesn't sound too big a deal, but it's actually an art. The branches that are being removed must be cut on the proper angle and chosen in a manner that will help balance the trees, and thought must be put into how the individual trees will grow and mature.

In mid-June the apple trees blossom. That's probably one of the most spectacular sights you'll ever see. The blossoms last for about 10 days before the petals fall to the ground and the fruit begins to grow. It is very important that the orchard is not disturbed during this time, probably the most important stage in the growing process. The bees collect the nectar from the flowers to make their honey, and as they go from flower to flower they cross-pollinate them. If this doesn't happen, the trees will not produce fruit.

From this point until the harvest the orchard is monitored for any pests, such as mice or caterpillars, or any disease that may damage the fruit or the trees themselves. Ongoing maintenance duties include lawn mowing, grooming walking trails, tightening tree supports, building picnic tables and planning the future of the orchard. An average apple tree will yield 200 to 300 pounds (100 to 150 kg) of apples in its prime (12 to 25 years old). As it ages, the tree will produce less and less fruit, so new trees have to be planted every year.

Marc has plans for more than just apples in his orchard. He has begun what he refers to as "Phase Two . . . the vineyard." He has planted around 250 grapevines, made up of five varietals, as an experiment to see which varietals flourish in the soil conditions and climate that he has to offer. The best varietals will be planted across the creek on the rolling hill that is currently being used by a local farmer to grow hay. There has also been mention of apple cider to go along with the wines.

roast honeycrisp apple, onion and squash soup with maple soy glaze

This recipe is inspired by the fall harvest. This is a time in PEI when there is a bounty of fresh food that is adored by chefs. Wide varieties of fruits and vegetables are in a state of perfect ripeness. Roasted squash and roasted apples are a perfect match. Unlike the flavour combinations in the pork belly recipe (page 110), this recipe ends up on the sweeter side. We've used an apple that's on the tart side, simply to help balance the whole dish. Enjoy! MAKES 5½ CUPS (1.4 L)

SOUP

one 2 lb (1 kg) butternut squash

3 Honeycrisp or McIntosh apples

1 large white onion

3 cloves garlic (peeled)

2 Tbsp (30 mL) canola oil

1 Tbsp (15 mL) chopped fresh thyme

1 cup (250 mL) apple juice

1 cup (250 mL) chicken stock (page 243)

1 cup (250 mL) whipping cream

2 Tbsp (30 mL) lemon juice

dash Tabasco sauce

salt and pepper

MAPLE SOY GLAZE

½ cup (125 mL) maple syrup

3 Tbsp (45 mL) soy sauce (my preference is for Oishi Sauce, a local PEI soy sauce)

Preheat the oven to 350°F (180°C).

Cut the squash in half lengthwise and place cut side down on a roasting pan. Roast the squash for 40 minutes, remove from the oven and allow to cool to room temperature. Peel off the skin and reserve the flesh. Leave the oven on while you do this.

Peel and roughly chop the apples and onion and place them in a bowl. Add the garlic cloves, canola oil and chopped thyme. Toss to coat. Place in the roasting pan that you used for the squash and roast in the oven for 20 minutes.

Transfer the roasted apple and onion mixture to a large (8 cup/2 L) saucepan. Add the reserved squash, apple juice, chicken stock and cream. Place the pot over medium-high heat, bring to a boil, then reduce the heat and simmer, uncovered, for 15 minutes.

Meanwhile, prepare the maple soy glaze. In a saucepan, bring the maple syrup and soy sauce to a gentle simmer and allow to reduce by half, 3 to 4 minutes. Let cool to room temperature.

Purée the soup with a handheld blender. Add the lemon juice, Tabasco sauce and salt and pepper to taste. Drizzle each serving with glaze.

maple and cider—glazed braised pork belly with spiced apple chutney

Chefs like to use apples in savoury dishes as well as sweet ones. In savoury dishes the chef must think about the sweetness of the apple and balance it with some sort of acid. In the case of the braised pork belly, the reduced wine becomes tart enough to offset the sweetness of the Cortland apple. SERVES 4—6

PORK BELLY

2 lb (1 kg) skinless pork belly

salt and pepper

½ cup (125 mL) sliced onion

3 Tbsp (45 mL) minced garlic

2 Tbsp (30 mL) minced fresh ginger

3 cups (750 mL) apple cider

3 cups (750 mL) chicken stock (page 243)

½ cup (125 mL) maple syrup

2 Tbsp (30 mL) soy sauce

CHUTNEY

1 cup (250 mL) finely diced onion

2 Tbsp (30 mL) salted butter

3 cups (750 mL) diced Cortland apples
  (peeled)

1 cup (250 mL) cider vinegar

¾ cup (185 mL) brown sugar (packed)

¼ cup (60 mL) raisins

2 Tbsp (30 mL) minced garlic

1 tsp (5 mL) yellow mustard seeds

1 tsp (5 mL) salt

pinch cayenne pepper

pinch ground cumin

pinch ground ginger

pinch dry mustard

1 tsp (5 mL) tomato paste

Preheat the oven to 325°F (160°C).

Cut the pork into 6 to 8 equal portions. Score the fat side of the pork with a sharp knife diagonally in two directions to create a diamond effect. Season the pork on both sides with salt and pepper, and sear (fat side down) in a large ovenproof braising pan for 3 to 4 minutes on each side, or until golden brown. Remove the pork from the pan and set aside.

Add the onion, garlic and ginger to the pan in which the pork was cooked, and sauté for 2 to 3 minutes. Add the reserved pork with the apple cider, chicken stock, maple syrup and soy sauce, cover, bring to a simmer then transfer to the oven for 1½ hours.

Meanwhile, prepare the chutney. In a large saucepan, sweat the onion in the butter over medium heat for 2 to 3 minutes. Add the apples and cook for an additional 4 to 5 minutes.

Add the remaining ingredients, except the tomato paste, and cook for 20 minutes over low heat, stirring occasionally. Stir in the tomato paste and cook for an additional 5 minutes, stirring again.

Remove the pork from the braising pan, tent it with foil, then reduce the cooking liquid by half on the stovetop. Slice the pork portions into small pieces or thin strips and serve with some reduced liquid and spiced apple chutney.

The apple chutney can be served hot or cold. It can be stored in the refrigerator for up to 1 week.

mom's apple pie with a twist

I know that everyone's mom makes the best apple pie, but I encourage you to try this one. It's actually my mom's pie but with a bit of a twist. Mom always made a single-crust pie and placed streusel on top of the apples instead of more crust. My only change has been to mix a little cream cheese into the filling. It's just one more dimension to a very simple dessert that is well loved by everyone. SERVES 6—8

1 unbaked 9-inch (23 cm) single deep-dish
   pie crust (page 235)
1 cup (250 mL) cream cheese (softened)
½ cup (125 mL) brown sugar (packed)
½ tsp (2 mL) ground mace
1 egg

½ tsp (2 mL) vanilla extract
4 cups (1 L) cored and thickly sliced
   Cortland apples
1 cup (250 mL) streusel topping (page 251)

Preheat the oven to 375°F (190°C). Line a 9-inch (23 cm) deep-dish pie plate with the unbaked pie crust.

Beat the cream cheese, sugar, mace, egg and vanilla to a creamy consistency. Place the apples in the pie shell and spoon the cheese mixture overtop. Top with the streusel and bake in the centre of the oven for 25 to 30 minutes. Let cool and serve with ice cream, cheddar cheese and/or whipped cream.

olde towne orchard varieties

- CORTLAND. The Cortland has a sweet flavour and a very white flesh and is an excellent dessert apple. This apple was developed at the New York State Agricultural Experiment Station in Geneva, New York, in 1898. It was named after nearby Cortland County in New York State. It is available from the fourth week of September.
- GINGER GOLD. This yellow-skinned apple became commercially available in 1980, although the original seeds date back to 1960. The Ginger Gold is the earliest variety to ripen. The flesh is a creamy yellow colour and resists browning better than other yellow varieties. The flavour is mild with a tart finish, making it ideal for most uses. It is available from the third week of September.

- HONEYCRISP. A combination of sweetness, tartness and crispy, firm texture make this a wonderful apple for eating raw. This is available from the fourth week of September.
- JONAGOLD. This apple is a cross between a Golden Delicious and a Jonathan apple. It is a large, delicious sweet apple with a thick skin and is great for eating raw or for cooking. It is available from the second week of October.
- MCINTOSH. Considered by many to be a great eating apple, it is also well suited for applesauce, cider and pies. It has a tart flavour and tender white flesh. It is available from the first week of October.

apple jelly

It seems as though we wait all summer long for apples, watching them grow on the trees. We taste them while they're still tart and realize we have to wait even longer. And then they're finally ripe, but the season goes very fast and we have to wait another year for the same experience!

Apples tend to store very well in cold rooms, but they still won't last forever. One of the greatest ways to preserve that wonderful apple taste is to make jelly. This recipe is sure to please. Try it with your favourite cheese. MAKES 4 CUPS (1 L)

18 McIntosh apples
3 cups (750 mL) sugar
one or two 3 fl oz (85 mL) packages liquid pectin (depending on ripeness of apples)

Roughly chop the whole apples (including the skin and core) and place them in a large saucepan. Add enough water to just cover the apples. Add the sugar and stir to incorporate.

Bring the mixture to a boil, reduce to a simmer and continue to cook the apples until they are soft.

Strain the cooking liquid through a fine-mesh sieve into a large container. Place the apples in a cheesecloth and sit them in a sieve placed over the container with the cooking liquid. Allow the juice from the apples to drain overnight into the container, then refrigerate. Do not squeeze the cheesecloth, as this will force pulp through the cloth and cause the jelly to be cloudy.

After the apples have been drained, discard the cheesecloth and apple flesh and seeds. Transfer the strained juices to a saucepan. Slowly bring to a boil, then reduce to a simmer and reduce the liquid by between one-half and three-quarters. The more the liquid is reduced, the greater the intensity of flavour, so it's up to you.

To test how well the jelly has set before you add any pectin, place a small portion in the fridge to cool. If the jelly has not fully set, gently warm it up and add 1 package of liquid pectin and perform the test again. If it still has not set, warm it up and add the second package of pectin.

Serve cool or at room temperature with your favourite cheeses, breads, etc. This keeps well in an airtight container in the refrigerator for up to 2 weeks.

blueberries

blue, blue berries

Wild blueberries have long been a part of the traditional culinary fabric of Prince Edward Island. Growing everywhere, from sporadic patches along our Confederation Trail to clusters along the edges of fields and ditches, this delicious little berry has truly flourished here on PEI. I remember spending hours picking these little beauties with my grandmother. Now there are numerous commercial operations on PEI growing and cultivating berries to be frozen and sold across North America or locally made into fruit wine. Blueberries have become part of a PEI chef's reserve.

Any culinary artist will tell you that the blueberry is an amazing fruit. Its colour is vibrant and its taste explosive. What's more, its antioxidant properties have raised it to the status of "superfood."

"Picked at just the right time, the berry just falls off the stem with the slightest nudge from my fingers." That's what my grandmother taught me as we wandered along the railway tracks (now Confederation Trail) behind my grandparents' farmhouse in Emerald, picking just the right amount of berries to make two pies for that evening's dessert. I would slip away to help my grandmother while my father and uncles were helping my grandfather take in the hay. I remember her telling me not to eat the green ones because they weren't ripe yet. And so the perfect cluster of ripe berries would explode in a burst of flavour in my mouth! I can still taste them today.

Picking that amount of berries was a tedious task, but it was time well spent with Grammy. And the end result was absolutely worth the effort. Her blueberry pies were legendary. I loved them so much that I would request blueberry pie instead of cake for my birthday. In fact, my wife carries on the tradition and makes me a blueberry pie for my birthday every single year. My love of blueberries and blueberry pie will probably stay with me for the rest of my life.

My first love as a chef is making desserts—taking me back to my days of working at the Inn at Bay Fortune. Chef Michael Smith would entrust me and my cold side crew to create a dessert menu that would evolve with the seasons as new ingredients became available. The local farmers would wait for my reaction when they delivered the fresh berries, their pride in their product shining on their faces!

Prince Edward Island has become a very lucrative blueberry-growing region in Eastern Canada. The sandy soil, level ground and relatively rock-free soil content make it very conducive to growing wild blueberries. The prime requirement is that the native wild blueberry be already present. Forest or scrub land with 20 percent blueberry coverage has been successfully developed into productive fields. Wild blueberries are spread by rhizomes, or underground runners, which produce new roots and stems. In a field where weeds are controlled, these runners can spread 15 inches (38 cm) in one growing season, although it takes several years to bring the land from an initial clearing to full plant coverage.

Most commercial production of wild blueberries is in Tignish, Wood Islands, Mount Stewart and Souris. Our ideal growing conditions have attracted international companies such as Jasper Wyman & Son of Maine, who set up a large production facility in West St. Peters (near Morell), contracting out to local commercial growers. They also make blueberry juice, but the best of the berries are individually quick frozen (IQF) and boxed for shipment off-Island. Hackett's is another Island company that processes blueberries in Tignish (the western end of the province) for the frozen berry market. I think it's funny that if I order blueberries from my national distributors I would likely get Wyman's blueberries from Prince Edward Island, which are also shipped across the entire continent.

Wild blueberries are attracting much attention for their antioxidant properties. They're everywhere— in muffins, wine, jam and preserves, cereals and yogurt. Blueberry wine, jam and preserves are all produced commercially on Prince Edward Island, giving an extra boost to this already thriving industry.

my grandmother's "happy birthday" blueberry pie

Of course, I had to give you this recipe; after all, it is my birthday cake! My grandmother would put the berries we picked into a two-quart ice cream container so that she would know exactly when she had enough berries to make two pies. MAKES 1 PIE

1 unbaked 10-inch (25 cm) double pie crust (page 235)
4 cups (1 L) fresh or frozen (do not thaw) wild blueberries
1 cup (250 mL) sugar
¼ cup (60 mL) all-purpose flour
pinch salt
1 Tbsp (15 mL) unsalted butter (cold)
sugar for top of crust

Preheat the oven to 400°F (200°C). Dampen a 10-inch (25 cm) pie plate with water, and line it with your unbaked pie crust.

In a large bowl combine the blueberries, sugar, flour and salt. Add this to the pastry shell.

Scatter the butter over the berry mixture, and cover the pie with the second piece of rolled pastry. Trim the edges and crimp them together with your thumbs and forefingers. Brush the top crust with water and sprinkle generously with granulated sugar. Use a pair of scissors to cut slits on the top crust.

Bake in the centre of the oven for 40 to 50 minutes or until the pastry is golden. Allow the pie to cool and set before serving. Serve with your favourite vanilla ice cream.

warm blueberry brown butter cakes

I bake this dessert with almost any fruit (strawberries, raspberries, apples, pears), depending on what's in season. Blueberries are my favourite, though! Here I combine them with the nuttiness of brown butter, back them up with some toasted pecans and finish them off with the heady aroma of freshly ground cardamom.

SERVES 8

½ lb (250 g) unsalted butter (browned,
  cooled—see tip below)
1½ cups (375 mL) sugar
4 eggs
1 tsp (5 mL) vanilla extract
2 cups (500 mL) fresh blueberries
¾ cup (185 mL) all-purpose flour
⅓ cup (80 mL) chopped pecans
1 tsp (5 mL) ground cardamom
pinch salt

Preheat the oven to 350°F (180°C). Grease eight 3-inch (8 cm) ramekins.

In a large bowl combine the cooled brown butter and sugar. Add the eggs and vanilla and mix until well combined.

Fold in the blueberries, flour, pecans, cardamom and salt. Do not overmix as this will make the cake a bit tough.

Pour the batter into the prepared ramekins until three-quarters full and place them on a baking sheet. Bake for 25 minutes in the centre of the oven. A toothpick should come out clean when the cakes are done.

Run a knife around the inside of the ramekins to loosen the cakes. Turn them out onto a wire rack and allow to cool slightly. These are best served warm with a generous dollop of maple syrup–doused whipped cream.

---

tip

Browning butter is really quite straightforward. Place ½ lb (250 g) of butter in a medium-sized saucepan. Allow the butter to melt completely without stirring. It will begin to bubble, cooking out its water content. After this it will come to the foaming stage. It's very easy to see when the butter is at this stage. It will start to smell very nutty, and the foam will start to change colour slightly. You will see small brown bits—caramelized milk solids—come up through the foam. When this happens, remove the pan from the heat and pour the butter into a metal bowl to cool.

When I called the very knowledgeable Edwin McKie of Howe Bay (near Souris) to check on the availability of this year's crop, he offered me a guided tour of one of his blueberry fields. My son, Finn, and I headed out early one Sunday morning to see where Edwin has about 25 acres in production. Edwin told us about the yield of his fields and the quality of this year's crop; he usually averages about 3,000 lb (1,500 kg) per acre in a good year. He knows the fields intimately and talks gently to the berries as he inspects the bushes for disease. He knows exactly what is going on in each of his 25 acres. Finn and I picked a basket of berries while we listened to Edwin tell his story. As chefs, we want to get to know the growers of the products we use, and we want to hear their stories. The farmers, fishers, producers, artists, winemakers, distillers, cheesemakers and gardeners are the people on the ground doing their work with a real passion, and we share that passion! When you know the story behind the products, you can fully appreciate what you put on your guests' plates. It inspires us to always respect ingredients and show them off in their best light.

Approximately 7,500 acres of PEI farmland produce 6.5 million pounds (2.95 million kg) of blueberries every year. Around 1 percent of these blueberries are sold fresh locally.

blueberry shortcake

If blueberries aren't in season, you can substitute whatever berry is in season. It's all good! We Islanders start with the first crop of strawberries and then continue on all summer long.

This recipe is made with nutmeg biscuits rather than traditional shortcake. MAKES 12 BISCUITS

JEFF'S NUTMEG BISCUITS
4 cups (1 L) all-purpose flour
2 Tbsp (30 mL) baking powder
½ cup (125 mL) sugar
2 Tbsp (30 mL) nutmeg
½ lb (250 g) unsalted butter or lard (cold)
2% milk
1 egg (gently beaten)
brown sugar

BERRIES
4 cup (1 L) fresh or frozen (do not thaw) blueberries
½ cup (125 mL) sugar
2 Tbsp (30 mL) Grand Marnier or amaretto

WHIPPED CREAM
4 cups (1 L) whipping cream
¼ cup (60 mL) sugar
¼ cup (60 mL) maple syrup
1 tsp (5 mL) ground cardamom

Preheat the oven to 400°F (200°C). Line a baking sheet with parchment paper.

For the biscuits, combine the dry ingredients, then cut in the butter until it is well incorporated and the mixture resembles rough breadcrumbs. Gradually add enough milk to bring the dough together. The dough should be a little moist and sticky.

Scatter flour on a clean work surface, then roll the dough out to a 1-inch (2.5 cm) thickness and cut it into the desired shape and size. I like circles or triangles for this.

Place the biscuit dough on the prepared baking sheet. Brush the tops of the biscuits with egg and sprinkle with brown sugar. Bake in the centre of the oven for 12 to 15 minutes or just until the biscuits are slightly golden. Cool on a cooling rack.

Meanwhile, place the berries in a bowl and toss them with the sugar. Add the Grand Marnier and let stand for 15 to 20 minutes to infuse the flavours.

For the whipped cream, whip together the cream, sugar, maple syrup and cardamom until soft peaks form. Be careful not to overwhip or you will lose volume.

To serve, cut a biscuit in half, spoon some berry mixture over one half, add a dollop of whipped cream and cap with the other biscuit half.

With today's field management practices, a top-producing blueberry field can produce as much as 8,000 lb (3,600 kg) per acre. That's a lot of blueberry pies!

blueberry and lemon spritzer

Island blueberries are the basis for Rossignol Estate Winery's blueberry wine, one of the first wines that local winemaker John Rossignol produced when he opened the winery in 1994. Using only local blue-berries, John ferments this perfectly balanced sweet nectar and ages it in large stainless steel tanks. John says: "Perfect served chilled with a fresh squeeze of lemon." A real summer hit! SERVES 1

ice
1 lemon (cut into wedges)
Rossignol blueberry wine
lemon-flavoured Perrier or soda water

Fill a large cocktail glass with ice, squeeze a wedge of lemon over the ice and add a fresh lemon wedge to the glass. Fill two-thirds of the glass with Rossignol blueberry wine and top with lemon Perrier or soda water. Stir well.

cranberries

berries from the bog

Cranberries are increasingly important here on the Island. PEI's cranberry bogs, which produce cranberries for export and local markets, are producing more berries every year. A local winery also makes a cranberry wine that pairs perfectly with a turkey dinner at any time of year. This nutrient-rich, attractive little berry really packs a punch!

Cranberries can be very tart or very sweet, depending on who's cooking. You may like them on the sweeter side or so tart that you have tears in your eye. But have you tried the dehydrated version? One brand of dried cranberries goes by the brand name Craisins: a "raisin" that is made by slowly removing the cranberry's water content. Some are infused with sugar and some are just as Nature intended. Either way they're tasty little treats with proven health benefits, loaded with antioxidants, anthocyanins and other nutritional goodies. From what I understand there are no negative consequences from eating too much of this adorable fruit.

Growing, cultivating and harvesting the cranberry are a lot of work, and I've had the opportunity to witness this very fascinating process. There are two types of harvesting: wet and dry. Dry harvesting simply means picking the berries by hand. It's time-consuming, costly and also relatively hard on the back. Wet harvesting is a little more complicated. Basically, the berries are harvested mechanically in an area that is flooded. The berries grow in "bogs"—very large, shallow, rectangular holes in the ground, surrounded by a ditch that is a little deeper than the bog. Imagine huge, empty swimming pools (but not made out of concrete). The cranberries grow on vines that are planted on the floor of this pool. Wet harvesting begins with the pumping of gallons and gallons of water from a spring-fed reservoir at the highest elevation, with the water draining from bog to bog. Gravity is less expensive and more environmentally friendly than a pump fuelled by petroleum or electricity.

The plants are completely submerged with enough water to allow the berries to float 16 to 24 inches (40 to 60 cm) above the plants. The farmer drives a specially equipped tractor, called a "beater," through the bog. The beater looks like a large reel mower that you might see on a golf course, but with no blades. The reels contain a series of horizontal pipes that rotate fairly quickly, but instead of cutting like a mower, they beat the berries off the vines. The berries then float to the surface, resulting in a red

sea of berries (which makes for some very interesting photography!).

Workers put on chest waders and walk through the bog with rakes and a unique set of netting that is used to gather the berries. With a worker at either end of this netting they pull the cranberries to what I refer to as a floating fenced area. The fenced area contains the berries and guides them to a conveyer system that carries them through a wash area before dropping them into the back of a truck. The trucks then transport the cranberries to a processing facility. The berries go through a vigorous second wash cycle and are then sorted. Most cranberries are sold to the beverage industry, but more and more of them are making their way into other food products.

Of course, it's not just about the harvest. There is work to be done from the time the ground thaws, right up until after the ground is frozen again in early winter. In late spring, once the ground has thawed, sprinklers are set in the bogs. When there is a risk of frost the farmer will spray water on the crops to keep the frost from causing any damage. Once the risk of frost has passed, the farmer will monitor the crops, weeding, spraying and nurturing during the summer and into the fall. Once the berries are ripe, the harvest begins. Post-harvest, the sprinklers come back out as the risk of frost returns. Finally, the bogs are slightly flooded and the water is allowed to freeze. This protects the plants during the winter months. The very last step is to spread sand over the ice-covered crop. The sand will eventually blend into the ground and help loosen the soil when it thaws in the spring.

At Mikita Farms in Farmington, Mike and Lolita Whitty harvest thousands of cranberries each year on Thanksgiving weekend, with their friends and neighbours lending a hand. After four to five days of work the berries are harvested and shipped off for further processing. Mike and Lolita are pioneers in the cranberry industry on PEI and were the very first farmers in the province to wet-harvest a cranberry crop.

beet and cranberry soup

From a chef's perspective, the cranberry is a gem. It can be used in both savoury and sweet dishes and adds colour and flavour. This soup, which is on the savoury side, is simply delightful. SERVES 4–6

1 medium red onion (small dice)
2 Tbsp (30 mL) olive oil
6 cups (1.5 L) vegetable stock or
    chicken stock (page 243)
1 lb (500 g) beets (small dice)
2 cups (500 mL) fresh or frozen
    (do not thaw) cranberries
2 Tbsp (30 mL) orange zest
¼ cup (60 mL) orange juice
1 Tbsp (15 mL) honey
pinch ground cloves

pinch ground allspice
salt and pepper
½ cup (125 mL) sour cream (optional)
    (low-fat if you prefer)

Gently sauté the diced onion in the olive oil until translucent, about 2 minutes. Add the stock, beets, cranberries, orange zest, orange juice, honey, cloves and allspice. Bring to boil, then reduce to a simmer, covered or uncovered (your preference), on medium-low heat for 1 hour.

Transfer to a blender and purée until smooth. Gradually add more stock if the soup seems too thick. Season to taste with salt and pepper and serve hot with a dollop of sour cream (if you like).

cranberry panna cotta

This recipe is Italian in origin and was originally made by combining cream, eggs and sugar and then setting them with gelatin. This version, with cranberries as the dominant flavour, uses buttermilk and no eggs and features a hint of orange. SERVES 8

1 cup (250 mL) fresh or frozen
(do not thaw) cranberries
⅓ cup (80 mL) sugar
2 Tbsp (30 mL) water
2 Tbsp (30 mL) orange zest
3½ cups (875 mL) whipping cream
4 tsp (20 mL) powdered gelatin

Place the cranberries, sugar, water and orange zest in a saucepan. Bring to a boil, then reduce to a simmer for 2 minutes. Cool slightly, add 3 cups (750 mL) of the cream and purée in a blender until smooth.

In a small saucepan, add the gelatin to the remaining ½ cup (125 mL) of cold buttermilk and allow to sit for 5 minutes to allow the gelatin to bloom. Gently warm over low heat to melt the gelatin. Fold the buttermilk-gelatin mix into the cranberry purée and pour into eight 2 fl oz (60 mL) ramekins. Refrigerate for at least 2 hours before serving to allow the gelatin to set.

cranberry and coconut tart

This is a great fall dessert. The tartness of the fresh cranberries is offset by the sweetened condensed milk. If you like, serve this with a scoop of your favourite ice cream or a dollop of whipped cream just to add a little more richness. SERVES 6–8

1 unbaked tart crust (page 235)

4 cups (1 L) unsweetened shredded coconut

2 cups (500 mL) fresh or frozen (do not thaw) chopped cranberries

1 can sweetened condensed milk

2 eggs (slightly beaten)

Preheat the oven to 350°F (180°C). Grease a 12-inch (30 cm) fluted tart pan.

Put the tart crust into the prepared tart pan and blind bake until the shell is lightly golden, about 20 minutes. Keep the oven on.

Combine the coconut, cranberries and condensed milk. Add the eggs and pour into the pastry shell. Cover with more coconut if you wish. Bake for 20 minutes. Let cool. Chill, uncovered, in the refrigerator until the pie is set.

old-fashioned cranberry sauce

CHEF AUSTIN CLEMENT

This is an old classic, and super-simple. It always seems to come out around the holidays, but it's awesome in a chicken sandwich any day. Orange and cranberry go great together, and if you follow this recipe exactly, the cranberries won't overcook. MAKES ABOUT 6 CUPS (1.5 L)

2 cups (500 mL) sugar
2 cups (500 mL) orange juice
4 cups (1 L) fresh or frozen cranberries

Dissolve the sugar in the orange juice and bring to a boil. Simmer, uncovered, for 10 minutes. Add the cranberries and simmer, covered, until the berries pop, about 5 minutes.

Remove from the heat and set aside. Allow to cool in the pot completely before lifting the lid. This will keep in the refrigerator in a tightly covered container for up to 7 days.

=== ⚬ tip ⚬ ===
Try adding a couple of tablespoons of this to your favourite biscuit recipe (or try the recipe on page 237). Simply add it when you're cutting in the butter.

cranberry chutney

Chutney is sweet, sour and sometimes a little spicy. It's made by stewing the main ingredients with some aromatics, vinegar (or other acidic liquid) and sugar. Chutney is usually served as a condiment—see page 110 for an apple chutney recipe to accompany pork belly. MAKES 1½ CUPS (375 ML)

1 small yellow onion (minced)

1 Cortland apple (peeled, cored, diced)

1 pear (your preference) (peeled, cored, diced)

2 Tbsp (30 mL) salted butter

1 cup (250 mL) fresh or frozen (do not thaw) cranberries

½ cup (125 mL) sugar

½ cup (125 mL) golden raisins

½ cup (125 mL) orange juice

1 jalapeño pepper (finely chopped, seeds removed)

1 Tbsp (15 mL) candied ginger, minced

pinch cinnamon

pinch ground cloves

pinch ground cardamom

pinch salt

Preheat a large saucepan and gently sauté the onion, apple and pear in the butter until golden brown. Add the cranberries, sugar, raisins, orange juice, jalapeño, ginger, spices and salt.

Bring to a boil, then reduce to a simmer and cook, uncovered, until the mixture thickens, 6 to 8 minutes.

Cool, cover and refrigerate for 3 hours before serving. This will keep for up to 7 days in the refrigerator.

cranberry curd

Curd has been made for many years using various fruits, although lemon curd is probably the most common and most popular. It was usually served at afternoon tea with scones as an alternative to jams or jellies. MAKES 1½ CUPS (375 ML)

2 cups (500 mL) fresh or frozen (do not
  thaw) cranberries
¼ cup (60 mL) water
¼ cup (60 mL) unsalted butter (softened)
1 cup (250 mL) sugar
4 eggs
1 Tbsp (15 mL) lemon juice

Place the cranberries and water in a saucepan, bring to a boil, then reduce to a simmer for 2 minutes. Remove from the heat, let cool slightly and purée in a blender until smooth.

Beat the butter and sugar until smooth and creamy, about 2 minutes. Add the eggs one at a time, beating well between additions. Add the lemon juice and cranberry purée. Transfer the mixture to a stainless steel mixing bowl or to the top of a double boiler. Do not worry if the mixture looks as though it has curdled at this point.

Prepare a large bowl of ice water.

Place the bowl with the egg mixture on a pot of simmering water and cook, stirring constantly with a whisk, until the mixture thickens, about 10 minutes. Remove from the heat, cool over the ice water and refrigerate in an airtight container for up to 3 days.

This is good in single-serving pre-baked tart shells (in the freezer section at most supermarkets), or in one large baked tart shell (recipe on page 235). Garnish with white chocolate and your favourite fresh berries.

gardens

backyard bounty

The home garden and market garden have a long history here on Prince Edward Island. Traditional agriculture always included a small market garden (i.e., something much smaller in scale, with a diversity of fresh produce usually sold directly to consumers) that helped supplement the main crops with fresh strawberries, corn or tomatoes, for example. But now, market-garden farm stands loaded with produce dot the countryside. For chefs, this means a wealth of fresh, local ingredients for our summer menus. Some of the best tomatoes I have ever eaten were grown by a local farmer here on PEI.

Prince Edward Island has often been referred to over the years as the million-acre farm. It actually has over 600,000 acres of farmland with around 1,700 farmers working the land to provide us with fresh vegetables, fruit and livestock. This chapter is all about what I think is the basic inspiration for farmers: the garden. And not just inspiration for farmers, but for all the chefs who use local produce. Every season there are many varieties of fresh vegetables ready to inspire a chef—even in the winter, with cellars and cold rooms filled with cold crops (such as carrots, turnips, onions and potatoes).

Most parents have had a bit of trouble getting their children to eat vegetables. Saying "vegetables are good for you" is usually not enough to convince the little rascals to eat them. Two ideas that might work . . . The first: to simply get super excited about the food that you're trying to get the kids to eat! That's what I do when I'm wearing my parenting

hat. Children are like little sponges, and they love to mimic their parents. The second idea is to plant a vegetable garden. Once children become involved in turning soil, planting seeds, weeding the garden and harvesting a small crop, they will probably be curious and enthusiastic, especially once they taste the sweet, tender/crisp garden vegetables they've grown by themselves.

Those who know me know that I tend to get very excited about ingredients. I have a few gardens on my property, and I like to involve my two children, Mackenzie and Matthew, who are nine and six. I'm thrilled to say that if you saw them at a birthday party, they'd be hanging out at the crudités platter, dipping and eating raw vegetables, while every other child would be eating potato chips.

You don't need to plant acres to carry out this experiment. Simply grow one or two cherry tomato plants in a large pot and set it on the patio. The children can watch the plants grow, water and weed them and finally harvest these little bursts of flavour. Nine times out of ten, the children will try them out and love them.

Something else that parents can try is to involve children in the cooking. Since sweetness is something children love, parents could get their children to sprinkle a little bit of sugar or honey on carrots before roasting them. But since carrots are naturally sweet, and roasting intensifies sweetness through caramelization, next time you can secretly roast them without sugar and they won't notice the difference!

buying produce
in season

Different vegetables mature at different times—chefs are always adjusting their menus! But you can trust that whatever produce is in season will excite a chef. This chart shows when the more common PEI vegetables are available for harvest.

ASPARAGUS	May, June
BEETS (BABY AND GREENS)	June, July, August, September
BROCCOLI	June, July, August, September
CABBAGE	June, July, August, September, October
CORN	August, September
CUCUMBERS	Late June, July, August, September, October
EGGPLANT	July, August, September, October
GREEN BEANS (OR YELLOW BEANS)	July, August, September
GREENS/LETTUCES	June, July, August, September
HERBS	June, July, August, September, October
PEPPERS	July, August, September, October
PUMPKINS	September, October
RHUBARB	June
SQUASH	September, October
TOMATOES	August, September, October

Most people out there know how to cook vegetables. They just need to learn a few more tricks to make their vegetables a touch more exciting. Cooking doesn't have to be about following a recipe; it's more fun if it's about experimenting and learning to identify what goes with what.

- ASPARAGUS. Blanch in salted boiling water, and cool in ice water. Toss with olive oil and place on the barbecue for just a couple of minutes to char. Toss with balsamic vinaigrette (page 246) and serve.
- BEETS. Wash and boil whole unpeeled beets in salted boiling water until tender, 15 to 20 minutes depending on their size. Cool, peel and dice. Sauté with butter, a splash of vinegar and a little fresh basil.
- BRUSSELS SPROUTS. Blanch Brussels sprouts in salted boiling water until tender, 4 to 6 minutes. Cool and reserve. Render 2 strips of diced bacon in a skillet. Add green onions and garlic and cook for 1 to 2 minutes. Add a splash of white wine and ¼ cup (60 mL) of whipping cream and bring to a simmer. Do not boil. Place the blanched Brussels sprouts in the simmering liquid and reduce until the cream thickens. Season and serve.
- CORN ON THE COB. Soak ears of corn, with the husk on, in cold water for 2 hours. Place them on a preheated barbecue for 30 minutes over medium-low heat, turning occasionally. The water in the husk will cause the corn to steam on the inside, and the charring of the husk will add a roasted aroma and flavour. Admittedly, it's a little messy to be husking the corn afterward, but it's certainly worth it.
- LEEKS. Cut and blanch leeks in boiling salted water. Cook 1 cup (250 mL) of blanched leeks with ¼ cup (60 mL) of whipping cream until the cream thickens. Bring to a boil, then reduce to a simmer for a few minutes. Season to taste and serve.
- SPINACH. Sauté a few minced green onions and a little minced garlic in some olive oil. Add some washed spinach, cover and steam for 2 to 3 minutes. Add a little butter, some chopped tomatoes, a splash of balsamic vinegar, salt and pepper, and serve.

bruschetta

A great way to enjoy fresh tomatoes is to make brus-
chetta. Crusty bread, aged balsamic, good olive oil and
ripe tomatoes are the necessities here. Mix and enjoy!

SERVES 8—10 AS AN APPETIZER

VINAIGRETTE
½ cup (125 mL) balsamic vinegar
2 tsp (10 mL) Dijon mustard
2 tsp (10 mL) minced green onion
2 tsp (10 mL) minced garlic
½ cup (125 mL) extra virgin olive oil
salt and pepper

BRUSCHETTA
¼ cup (60 mL) salted butter (softened)
1 Tbsp (15 mL) minced garlic
20 slices baguette
4 ripe Roma tomatoes (diced, skin left on)
¼ cup (60 mL) fresh basil leaves (sliced)
salt and pepper
grated Parmesan cheese as needed

For the vinaigrette, combine the balsamic vinegar, mustard, green onion and garlic in a medium-sized stainless steel bowl. Slowly add the olive oil in a steady stream, whisking constantly. Season to taste with salt and pepper and set aside.

For the bruschetta, combine the butter and garlic and set aside. Toast the baguette slices in the oven until golden brown and spread with the garlic butter.

Place the tomatoes and basil in a stainless steel bowl and toss with just enough vinaigrette to coat. Season to taste with salt and pepper. Spoon the mixture onto the toast and top with grated Parmesan.

Serve immediately!

Any excess vinaigrette can be refrigerated for up to 1 week.

beefsteak tomato and pea shoot salad with basil and aged cheddar

Make sure you have perfectly ripe tomatoes and tender pea shoots for this. It will make all the difference in the world. SERVES 4

2 Tbsp (30 mL) balsamic vinegar
2 Tbsp (30 mL) grainy mustard
2 Tbsp (30 mL) minced onion
1 Tbsp (15 mL) minced garlic
¼ cup (60 mL) extra virgin olive oil
salt and pepper
4 medium-sized ripe garden
  beefsteak tomatoes
2 cups (500 mL) fresh young pea shoots
1 cup (250 mL) chopped fresh basil leaves
1 cup (250 mL) snipped chives
4 cloves garlic (roasted and chopped)
½ cup (125 mL) aged white cheddar (shaved)

In a bowl, combine the vinegar, mustard, onion and garlic. Slowly add the olive oil by pouring it in a steady stream and whisking constantly to create an emulsion. Season with salt and pepper as desired.

Thinly slice the tomatoes, arrange them on a plate and season to taste with salt and freshly cracked black pepper.

Toss the pea shoots, basil and chives with enough vinaigrette to coat all the leaves. Place this overtop the tomatoes and sprinkle with roasted garlic and shaved cheddar.

grilled halibut with summer salsa

Salsa is basically a mixture of fruit and/or vegetables, so it follows that for great salsa, you should use fruits and vegetables that are at the perfect point of maturity or ripeness. SERVES 4

SALSA

2 Tbsp (30 mL) balsamic vinegar
1 Tbsp (15 mL) honey
1 Tbsp (15 mL) lemon zest
1 Tbsp (15 mL) lemon juice
¼ cup (60 mL) finely chopped fresh cilantro
3 Tbsp (45 mL) olive oil
½ cup (125 mL) small-diced tomatoes
¼ cup (60 mL) finely diced peaches
  (peeled, pitted)
¼ cup (60 mL) finely diced pears
  (peeled, pitted)
¼ cup (60 mL) finely diced red bell pepper
¼ cup (60 mL) finely diced red onion
1 medium jalapeño pepper (seeded
  and finely diced)
salt and pepper

HALIBUT

four 5 oz (150 g) halibut portions
olive oil
salt and pepper
2 Tbsp (30 mL) lemon juice

Begin with the salsa. Combine the vinegar, honey, lemon zest and juice and cilantro in a mixing bowl. Slowly add the olive oil, whisking constantly to create an emulsion. Add the remaining ingredients, stir thoroughly and season with salt and pepper to taste. Set aside until needed. (The salsa will keep in the refrigerator for up to 3 days.)

Preheat the barbecue or grill to medium-high heat. Drizzle the halibut on both sides with olive oil and season with salt and pepper. Gently place the fish on the grill and cook for 2 to 3 minutes on each side. Drizzle each side with freshly squeezed lemon juice when you turn the fish.

Serve with the salsa.

coleslaw

Coleslaw is a very common side dish, and you can often buy it already prepared. It's really not that hard to make, though. Some like it tangy, and some like it sweet; this one is somewhere in the middle. If you prefer a little more zip, just add more vinegar. SERVES 8

6 cups (1.5 L) shredded green cabbage
1 cup (250 mL) shredded carrot
3 Tbsp (45 mL) chopped fresh parsley
¼ cup (60 mL) cider vinegar
3 Tbsp (45 mL) sugar
1 Tbsp (15 mL) lemon juice
1 cup (250 mL) mayonnaise
salt and pepper

Combine the cabbage, carrot and parsley in a mixing bowl and set aside.

In a separate bowl, mix the vinegar, sugar and lemon juice, stirring to dissolve the sugar. Add this mixture to the mayonnaise and stir until combined.

Add the mayonnaise mixture to the cabbage mixture and mix until the cabbage is well coated. Season to taste with salt and pepper.

Refrigerate for at least 1 hour before serving. This will keep in the refrigerator for up to 3 days.

beet relish

I got this recipe from my father-in-law and have used it in just about every restaurant I have worked in. It is extremely simple, quick to make and did I men-tion delicious? MAKES ABOUT FOUR 2-CUP (500 ML) MASON JARS

6 cups (1.5 L) cooked, peeled and grated
 beets (let cool before grating)
1 cup (250 mL) cider vinegar
4 cups (1 L) sugar
1 tsp (5 mL) ground ginger
½ tsp (2 mL) ground cloves
½ tsp (2 mL) ground allspice

Combine all the ingredients in a small Dutch oven and bring to a boil. Reduce the heat and simmer, uncovered, for 20 minutes.

Bottle the mixture in sterile jars, leave ½ inch (1 cm) headspace and cover with lids while still hot.

Submerge the filled, covered jars in boiling water and process for 10 minutes. Cool at room tempera-ture and make sure the lids pop (see page 161).

Serve the relish with goat cheese and crackers, meats, new potatoes or at any meal! Properly canned beets will keep for 6 months in a cool, dark place. Opened jars will keep in the refrigerator for up to 2 weeks.

stewed rhubarb

When they hear rhubarb, most people think dessert. You can certainly serve this stewed rhubarb with a sweet biscuit to make a simple rhubarb shortcake, but try adding two peeled, diced apples and serving this with grilled pork; or adding a handful of pitted cherries and serving with grilled chicken. MAKES ABOUT 3 CUPS (750 ML)

6 cups (1.5 L) chopped fresh rhubarb
  (1-inch/2.5 cm pieces)
1 cup (250 mL) sugar
2 Tbsp (30 mL) orange zest
¼ cup (60 mL) orange juice

Place the rhubarb, sugar, orange zest and juice in a saucepan. Bring to a boil, reduce to a simmer and cook, uncovered, for 7 to 8 minutes, stirring occasionally.

Cool and serve. This keeps in the refrigerator for up to 3 days.

pickles

Pickles are a long-time favourite of mine. I think it's interesting that so many recipes have been created expressly for preserving. Years ago, the lack of refrigeration and freezing meant we had to prepare foods in a certain way to preserve them. Now we tend to make them because we just love them that way, pickles probably being the best example. We have two types of pickle recipes in this section, the first involving a whole process of cooking, canning and storing for later consumption. The second type is simply submerging vegetables in an acidic solution for a short period of time and then consuming them right away.

pickled onions

SERVES 4

- **1 medium onion (finely sliced)**
- **1½ tsp (7.5 mL) salt**
- **⅓ cup (80 mL) cider vinegar**
- **¼ cup (60 mL) water**
- **3 Tbsp (45 mL) sugar**
- **1 clove garlic (cut in half)**
- **½ tsp (2 mL) yellow mustard seeds**
- **½ tsp (2 mL) prepared mustard (your preference)**
- **pinch celery seed**

Place the onion in a bowl and sprinkle with 1 tsp (5 mL) of the salt. Let stand for 1 hour. Drain and rinse in cold water.

Combine the vinegar, water, sugar, garlic, mustard seeds, prepared mustard, celery seed and remaining salt in a saucepan. Bring to a boil, then reduce to a simmer for 2 minutes. Stir in the onion and simmer for another 3 minutes. Cool, cover and refrigerate for 3 hours before serving. This will keep well for 1 week in the refrigerator.

pickled red onions

SERVES 4–6

- **1 medium red onion (halved and thinly sliced)**
- **½ cup (125 mL) red wine vinegar**
- **½ cup (125 mL) water**
- **2 Tbsp (30 mL) sugar**
- **1 bay leaf**

Place the sliced onion in a medium-sized, heatproof bowl. Place the vinegar, water, sugar and bay leaf in a saucepan. Bring to a boil, reduce to a simmer and stir until the sugar is dissolved. Remove from the heat and pour over the onion slices. Set aside to cool at room temperature and marinate for at least 30 minutes. Discard the bay leaf. Cover and refrigerate for 3 hours before serving. This will keep well for 1 week in the refrigerator.

pickled mushrooms

MAKES 2 CUPS (500 ML)

- **2 medium onions (thinly sliced into rings)**
- **1½ cups (375 mL) red wine vinegar**
- **1½ cups (375 mL) water**
- **½ cup (125 mL) brown sugar (packed)**
- **¼ cup (60 mL) pickling salt**
- **1 tsp (5 mL) crushed dried tarragon**
- **1 lb (500 g) white button mushrooms (cleaned, trimmed, kept whole)**

Combine the onion rings, red wine vinegar, water, brown sugar, pickling salt and tarragon in a saucepan and bring to a boil. Add the mushrooms and simmer, uncovered, for 5 minutes.

Using a slotted spoon, lift the mushrooms and onion rings from the pickling liquid. Reserve the liquid, keeping it hot.

Pack the vegetables in hot, clean Mason jars, leaving ½ inch (1 cm) headspace.

Cover with hot pickling liquid, again leaving ½ inch (1 cm) headspace, and cover with clean lids. Submerge the filled, covered jars in boiling water and process for 10 minutes.

Cool at room temperature and make sure the lids pop. When hot foods cool, they contract or shrink. The pop is the sound of the lid being pulled down by the cooling process. If the lid does not pop, you should refrigerate the mushrooms and use within 1 week. If it does pop, then you have made a good seal on the lid, and the mushrooms can be stored for up to 3 months.

spicy pickled cucumbers with wasabi
SERVES 4–6

> 5 baby cucumbers
> 2 tsp (10 mL) coarse salt
> ¼ cup (60 mL) seasoned rice vinegar
> ½ tsp (2 mL) wasabi powder
> ½ tsp (2 mL) soy sauce

Cut the cucumbers into long, thin strips about ⅛ inch (3 mm) thick and place them in a colander. Sprinkle them with salt and allow to drain for 15 minutes. Rinse the cucumbers under cold running water and allow to drain again. Pat dry with paper towel.

Mix together the vinegar, wasabi powder and soy sauce until the wasabi is dissolved. Toss the cucumbers with the sauce, cover and refrigerate until you are ready to serve. These pickles can be refrigerated for up to 1 week.

spicy pickled carrots and asparagus
MAKES 2 CUPS (500 ML)

> 2 lb (1 kg) asparagus (trimmed)
> 4 cups (1 L) water
> 3 cups (750 mL) cider vinegar
> ½ cup (125 mL) sugar
> 10 sprigs fresh thyme
> 3 Tbsp (45 mL) minced garlic
> 1 Tbsp (15 mL) sea salt
> 1 Tbsp (15 mL) yellow mustard seeds
> 1½ tsp (7.5 mL) freshly ground black pepper
> 1½ tsp (7.5 mL) crushed chili flakes
> 1 lb (500 g) carrots (peeled, thinly sliced)
> 1 small onion (thinly sliced and
>   cut into rings)

Prepare a bowl of ice water.

Blanch the asparagus in salted boiling water for 1 minute, then shock in the ice water for a few minutes. Combine the 4 cups (1 L) water with the vinegar, sugar, thyme, garlic, salt, mustard seeds, pepper and chili flakes. Bring to a boil, reduce to a simmer and cook, uncovered, for 10 minutes.

Place the carrots and onion in a bowl and cover with the hot pickling liquid. Allow to cool to room temperature and add the asparagus. Cover and refrigerate for at least 24 hours. This will keep in an airtight container for up to 1 week in the refrigerator.

continued . . .

PICKLES *continued*

mustard pickles

This recipe comes from my wife's family. These pickles are fantastic with fish cakes and complete any pork roast dinner. Most cellars on Prince Edward Island have at least one variation of mustard pickles on the shelf.—J.M. MAKES EIGHT 2-CUP (500 ML) MASON JARS

16 cups (4 L) small-diced cucumbers (peeled)

4 cups (1 L) small-diced onion

2 cups (500 mL) small cauliflower florets

1 cup (250 mL) pickling salt

1¼ cups (310 mL) all-purpose flour

6 cups (1.5 L) cider vinegar (must be cold)

7 cups (1.75 L) sugar

¼ cup (60 mL) dry mustard

2 Tbsp (30 mL) turmeric

1 Tbsp (15 mL) celery seeds

1 cup (250 mL) finely diced red bell pepper

In a large bowl, toss the cucumbers, onion and cauliflower in the salt to coat. Cover with just enough water to submerge. Let the vegetables soak overnight but no more than 12 hours. The next morning, drain the vegetable mixture and rinse off all the salt. Set aside.

Dissolve the flour in just enough vinegar to make a smooth, pourable paste. It is important to remove any lumps by passing the mixture through a sieve. Set aside.

In a large Dutch oven or pickling pot, dissolve the sugar in the remaining vinegar with the spices and bring to a boil.

Remove from the heat and slowly whisk in the flour mixture. The mixture will quickly begin to thicken, but don't panic. Whisk until all the flour is incorporated and there are no lumps.

Add the rinsed vegetable mixture and return to a boil. Let this mixture boil for 5 minutes. Add the red pepper, boil for 1 more minute then remove from the heat.

Transfer the pickles straight from the boiling pot into hot sterile jars, and process the jars in a boiling water bath for 10 minutes, following home-canning procedures. If you are not going to can them, they can be kept refrigerated for 10 days.

chili sauce

This is a great accompaniment to Acadian Meat Pie (page 29). I can remember eating this with meat pie back when I was a youngster. Fresh tomatoes are essential for this recipe.—J.M. MAKES SIX 1-CUP (250 ML) MASON JARS

7 cups (1.75 L) diced ripe tomatoes
   (skin left on)
½ cup (125 mL) diced onion
1 cup (250 mL) diced apple (Cortland
   or Spartan would work well here)
1½ cups (375 mL) diced celery
1 cup (250 mL) white vinegar
1½ cups (375 mL) sugar
2 tsp (10 mL) sea salt
½ tsp (2 mL) cayenne pepper
½ tsp (2 mL) ground cloves
1 tsp (5 mL) ground allspice

Combine all the ingredients in a large stockpot. Bring to a boil, then reduce the heat and simmer, uncovered, for 1½ hours.

Pour the hot mixture into hot, sterilized Mason jars and process the jars in a boiling water bath for 10 minutes, following home-canning procedures. Let the jars cool on the counter. The lids will seal as they cool. (Listen for the pop!)

Store in your cold room or in a cool place. Once open, the jar can be kept in the refrigerator for up to 2 months.

mushrooms

foraging with a master

Chanterelles! Aah, what bliss. These golden forest gems are a true delicacy. The golden chanterelle litters the softwood forests that dot the landscape of Prince Edward Island. Every enthusiast has a secret location that produces these tasty little yellow mushrooms every year. We chefs love when the first crops of chanterelles hit the prep table. During chanterelle season, Chef Hans Anderegg can be found knocking on the back door to sell that day's harvest.

The chanterelles arrive in early to late July and stay until late October. In the restaurant we showcase several edible varieties of local wild mushrooms: not just chanterelles, but also shaggy manes, puffballs, lobster mushrooms, porcini (also known as king bolete) and hen of the woods. At one particular get-together we used seven different types of mushroom that we had foraged in the afternoon for a wild mushroom ragout. We served it with braised Island lamb shoulder and some fresh garden sage. We really hit the jackpot that day.

During the peak mushroom season, when I was working at the Inn at Bay Fortune, we were hosting a mushroom brunch one Sunday morning. For this brunch, we had the guests forage for the mushrooms that were going to be part of the meal. It was our first venture of this type. Mushroom specialist Katherine Clough (from the PEI Department of Agriculture) and Chef Hans Anderegg joined us with a slew of guests who were intrigued by the idea of foraging for their own meal. We set out early in the morning,

and I led the group down to my "secret" patch near Back Beach. We wove our way through the woods in small groups, working our way back towards the Inn. We were scoring all kinds of mushrooms, especially chanterelles and porcinis. I strayed away from the group and was delighted to come across six giant lobster mushrooms. So-named because of its red colour, the lobster mushroom actually starts off as a parasite fungus that grows on a host mushroom, usually a bolete variety, transforming it into a lobster mushroom. They are dense and need to be cooked to be palatable. As I emerged from the brush, cradling these six giants in my arms, I drew a gasp of amazement from both Hans and Katherine. It was an amazing find for the day and was a real crowd-pleaser, since everyone had come for the experience of mushroom hunting. We couldn't have had a better day.

After a few hours in the woods we picked up our baskets and headed back to the Inn to prepare a mushroom brunch. All the dishes we prepared were made with the freshly picked mushrooms: wild mushroom frittata with white truffle oil; wild mushroom strudel with garden spinach sauce; lobster mushroom stir-fry with sesame and hoisin; cheddar gnocchi with chanterelle mushroom, peas and basil; wild mushroom ragout with garden sage; and wild mushroom pizza. We ate and breathed mushrooms for the next two hours, and by the end, we were stuffed—just like a stuffed mushroom!

One afternoon in early September we got a call from Mary and Max, friends of ours who own Woodville Mills Country Inn. They were very excited to tell us about the hen of the woods mushrooms that they had found growing around the 150-year-old oak trees scattered around their heritage property. We hopped in the truck and sped off to retrieve our prize.

We've had many calls out of the blue like that one. Once we got a call that a fisher had caught two sturgeons. (Those ancient fish were awesome. What a treat for our guests that night!) So this time, we arrived at Woodville Mills and were met by Max, who took us to a large oak tree on the front lawn of the property to show us a rather special mushroom. This mushroom was huge. It was about 2 feet (60 cm) in diameter and was made up of a "clustered mass of greyish brown, fleshy spoon-shaped caps with whitish pores, and lateral, white stalks branching from a compound base" (from the *National Audubon Society Field Guide to North American Mushrooms*).

Hen of the woods mushrooms can grow to anywhere between 5 and 100 pounds (2.2 to 45 kg). This one was a beauty. My mind started to race with ideas for taking this gem of a mushroom from forest to plate: hen of the woods mushroom risotto to be served with smoked wild boar, truffle-buttered garden chard, rosemary jus and crisp sweet potatoes. I am salivating just thinking about it. We bartered a Chef's Tasting Menu for their group the next time they made it back to the Inn at Bay Fortune.

It's an amazing feeling being so connected to the local community around us.

mushroom production on the island

Commercially, two varieties of mushrooms are grown on Prince Edward Island: white button mushrooms, grown at Rol-Land Farms in Freetown (western PEI), and shiitakes, grown in Fortune (eastern PEI). Commercial mushroom production is a very sterile process. Mushroom rhizomes are grown in bales of sterile straw and horse manure.

The bales are placed in a carefully controlled environment, with temperature, light and humidity, for example, all being closely monitored so that the fungus will produce the optimum mushrooms. Mushrooms are cut off these bales, graded, packaged and sold to markets off-Island. Hundreds of thousands of mushrooms are grown each year.

crab-stuffed mushroom caps

This is a very quick and simple hors d'oeuvre that your guests will be sure to love. MAKES 24 MUSHROOM CAPS

1 cup (250 mL) cooked crabmeat
1 Tbsp (15 mL) extra virgin olive oil
2 Tbsp (30 mL) minced green onion
1 Tbsp (15 mL) minced garlic
¼ cup (60 mL) dry white wine
3 Tbsp (45 mL) chopped fresh herbs
   (a mix of parsley, chives, tarragon)
salt and pepper
24 white button mushrooms (cleaned
   and stems removed)

Preheat the oven to 375°F (190°C). Butter a rimmed baking sheet.

Squeeze the juice from the crabmeat and reserve.

Heat the olive oil in a skillet over medium heat. Add the green onion and garlic. Deglaze the skillet with the white wine and add the reserved crab juice.

Reduce the liquid by three-quarters, then add the herbs and crabmeat. Mix well and season to taste.

Stuff each mushroom cap with about 1 Tbsp (15 mL) of the crab mixture. Any excess crab mix can be frozen for later use.

Place the stuffed mushrooms on the prepared baking sheet and bake for 10 to 12 minutes.

Serve immediately.

wild mushroom frittata

I make this sometimes over an open fire when I am hiking in the woods foraging for mushrooms. I always pack a few supplies so that I can have lunch along the way. SERVES 4

¼ cup (60 mL) olive oil
½ cup (125 mL) minced red onion
4 cups (1 L) edible wild mushrooms
   (I like to use chanterelles and porcinis)
1 cup (250 mL) diced zucchini
8 eggs (beaten)
1 cup (250 mL) grated aged Gouda
¼ cup (60 mL) minced fresh sage
white truffle oil
salt and pepper

Over an open fire, preheat a cast iron skillet.

Add the olive oil, followed by the minced onion and cook until soft. Add the mushrooms and zucchini. Sauté until soft and golden brown. Add the eggs and stir until the eggs are almost fully cooked. Add the cheese, sage and a few drops of the white truffle oil. Season to taste with salt and pepper.

Eat directly from the cast iron pan.

The staff "family meals" are very important to any kitchen team. We usually start our day at 9 a.m. with breakfast at the chef's table. In one restaurant where I worked we would have whatever was on the go from the breakfast cook. He would use the wild mushrooms in season in an omelette as his breakfast special. We would go over the day's prep list, organize the things we needed, sort out what was coming in from the garden (we usually started our morning with a quick trip through the garden to touch base with the girls who worked there) and in general talk about food. There was a lot of collaboration and brainstorming in these morning sessions as we prepared for the day. The great food helped us through!

chicken, pesto and chanterelle mushroom pizza

This pizza was the first thing we had for one of the "family meals" at the restaurant the day chanterelles first arrived in the kitchen. And trust me, we didn't skimp on the mushrooms! MAKES TWO 12-INCH (30 CM) FLAT-CRUST PIZZAS • SERVES 6

1 recipe pizza dough (page 236)
6 Tbsp (90 mL) basil pesto
3 cups (750 mL) shredded mozzarella
1 small red onion (thinly sliced)
1 cup (250 mL) chanterelle mushrooms
   (sautéed in unsalted butter)
½ cup (125 mL) medium-diced
   red bell pepper
6 slices bacon (cooked and chopped)
four 4 oz (125 g) chicken breasts (seasoned
   with salt and pepper and grilled)

Preheat the oven to 425°F (220°C).

Divide the pizza dough in two and spread each piece over a 12-inch (30 cm) greased pizza pan or stone.

Spread 3 Tbsp (45 mL) of pesto over each crust and sprinkle with a thin layer of the shredded cheese. Scatter red onion liberally overtop and then add the chanterelles, red pepper and bacon. Slice the chicken breasts into thin slices and place them on each pizza in a circular pattern. Top with the remaining cheese.

Bake for 20 to 25 minutes, until the cheese and the pizza edges are golden brown and crisp.

Slice each pizza in 6. Serve.

chanterelle, chicken and bean salad

This recipe shows off our beloved chanterelle with a starring role in a summer salad that also makes great use of our garden's green beans and thyme. SERVES 6

SALAD
six 4 oz (125 g) chicken breasts
¼ cup (60 mL) olive oil
13 oz (400 g) chanterelle mushrooms
¼ cup (60 mL) unsalted butter (softened)
salt and pepper
chopped fresh thyme and summer
    savory to taste
10 oz (300 g) green beans (cut in 1½-inch/
    4 cm long pieces)
6 slices rye bread

VINAIGRETTE
6 Tbsp (90 mL) olive oil
3 Tbsp (45 mL) balsamic vinegar
2 small shallots (finely diced)
2 cloves garlic (finely diced)
salt and pepper

Season the chicken breast with salt and pepper then sear in a pan with the olive oil. Let cool and cut it into thin strips.

Clean the chanterelles (if necessary) and cut the larger ones in half or into 4 pieces. Add the butter to the pan you used for the chicken and sauté the mushrooms for 3 to 4 minutes. Season to taste with salt and pepper and the fresh herbs.

Prepare a bowl of ice water.

Meanwhile boil the green beans in salted water until tender. Remove them from the pan and place them immediately in the ice water to stop the cooking process.

For the vinaigrette, add all the ingredients to a bowl and mix well with a whisk.

Add the chicken strips, chanterelles and beans to the vinaigrette and let marinate for at least 20 minutes. Season to taste with salt and ground pepper. Meanwhile, lightly toast the 6 slices of rye bread.

Divide the topping among the toasted slices of rye bread. Garnish with a sprig of thyme. Serve.

mushrooms on the side six ways

Here is a selection of ways to prepare mushrooms, each one a perfect accompaniment to just about any main dish. I've said it before, and I'll say it again: mushrooms are a wonderful, versatile ingredient that no chef should be without.

mushrooms in a whiskey bacon cream sauce

This would be a great accompaniment to pork, chicken or turkey. SERVES 6—8 AS A SIDE DISH

1 cup (250 mL) chopped bacon
1 cup (250 mL) sliced shiitake mushrooms
1 cup (250 mL) hand-torn oyster
   mushrooms
1 cup (250 mL) sliced white button
   mushrooms
½ cup (125 mL) small-diced red onion
2 Tbsp (30 mL) chopped fresh parsley
1 Tbsp (15 mL) minced garlic
1 fl oz (30 mL) whiskey
1 cup (250 mL) whipping cream
salt and pepper

Preheat a large stainless steel skillet on the stove. Add the bacon with a splash of water. When the bacon is cooked, add the mushrooms and sauté for 1 minute.

Add the onion, parsley and garlic and sauté for 1 minute. Add the whiskey and flambé. Add the cream and bring to a simmer, stirring occasionally. Do not boil. Allow the cream to reduce to a consistency that binds the mushrooms, 5 to 7 minutes. Season to taste with salt and pepper.

mushroom skewers

This is awesome with a nice barbecued steak. SERVES 4 AS A SIDE DISH

1 clove garlic (peeled)
1 Tbsp (15 mL) chopped fresh basil
1 Tbsp (15 mL) chopped fresh oregano
1 Tbsp (15 mL) chopped fresh thyme
1 Tbsp (15 mL) chopped green onion
¼ cup (60 mL) canola oil
8 small cremini mushrooms
8 chunks red bell pepper (1 medium
   pepper, medium dice)
8 chunks red onion (½ medium onion,
   medium dice)
8 chunks zucchini (1 small zucchini,
   medium dice)
sea salt and pepper

Soak 4 bamboo skewers in water for 1 hour before you begin to prevent the skewers from burning.

Using a handheld blender, purée the garlic, basil, oregano, thyme and green onion in the canola oil. Allow the resulting herb oil to sit for 30 minutes.

Place 2 pieces of each vegetable onto a skewer, alternating each type. Place the finished skewers in a baking pan or dish and brush evenly with the prepared herb oil. Season to taste with salt and pepper.

Preheat the charbroiler or grill to 400°F (200°C).

Cook the skewers for about 1 minute on each side. Serve immediately.

continued . . .

grilled portobello mushrooms

Portobellos are often used as a meat substitute in a vegetarian burger. SERVES 4 AS A SIDE DISH

2 cloves garlic (peeled)
2 Tbsp (30 mL) chopped fresh basil
2 Tbsp (30 mL) chopped fresh oregano
2 Tbsp (30 mL) chopped fresh thyme
2 Tbsp (30 mL) chopped green onion
½ cup (125 mL) canola oil
2 large portobello mushrooms
sea salt and pepper

Using a handheld blender, purée the garlic, basil, oregano, thyme and green onion with the canola oil. Allow the resulting herb oil to sit for about 30 minutes.

Using a teaspoon, remove the black gills from the mushrooms, then peel the skin from their top sides. Marinate the mushrooms in the herb oil for 2 hours. (Any longer will make them go mushy.) Remove, pat dry with a paper towel and season to taste with salt and pepper.

Preheat a charbroiler or grill to 400°F (200°C).

Cook the mushrooms for 1 to 2 minutes on each side. Remove from the heat, cut the mushrooms as desired and serve with a main course.

balsamic marinated mushrooms

An Italian staple, balsamic vinegar, adds a nice balance of sweet and sour to this dish. MAKES 2 CUPS (500 ML)

1 cup (250 mL) small-diced red onion
½ cup (125 mL) extra virgin olive oil
½ cup (125 mL) balsamic vinegar
2 Tbsp (30 mL) chopped fresh basil
1 Tbsp (15 mL) minced garlic
sea salt and pepper
1 Tbsp (15 mL) canola oil
3 cups (750 mL) quartered white button mushrooms

Combine the onion, olive oil, balsamic vinegar, basil, garlic, and salt and pepper to taste in a large mixing bowl.

Preheat a large skillet on the stove. Add the canola oil to the pan and quickly sauté the mushrooms, being careful not to brown them.

Add the hot mushrooms to the marinade in the mixing bowl and soak for 1 hour. Drain off the excess liquid and serve. The mushrooms can be refrigerated for up to 2 days once cool.

continued . . .

MUSHROOMS ON THE SIDE SIX WAYS *continued*

asian marinated shiitake mushrooms

The shiitake is native to Japan but is now commercially available worldwide. Shiitakes have a wonderful flavour and have an interesting texture when cooked. MAKES 3 CUPS (750 ML)

3 cups (750 mL) sliced fresh shiitake
   mushrooms
½ cup (125 mL) thinly sliced leek
½ cup (125 mL) thinly sliced red onion
½ cup (125 mL) thinly sliced carrot
½ cup (125 mL) thinly sliced celery
1 Tbsp (15 mL) canola oil
¼ cup (60 mL) sesame seed oil
¼ cup (60 mL) Oishi Sauce (or your
   favourite soy sauce)
1 Tbsp (15 mL) minced garlic
1 Tbsp (15 mL) minced ginger
2 whole star pods anise
1 Tbsp (15 mL) chopped fresh cilantro
pinch dried chili flakes

In a large skillet, sauté the mushrooms, leek, onion, carrot and celery in the canola oil. Transfer the hot vegetables to a mixing bowl. Add all the remaining ingredients and stir thoroughly. Allow the mushrooms to marinate for 1 hour.

The mushrooms can be refrigerated once cool and can be kept for up to 2 days.

sautéed mushrooms with garlic and onions

This is a staple side dish for any steak lover! MAKES 1 CUP (250 ML)

2 Tbsp (30 mL) canola oil
3 cups (750 mL) sliced white
   button mushrooms
2 Tbsp (30 mL) minced green onion
1 Tbsp (15 mL) minced garlic
1 Tbsp (15 mL) chopped fresh parsley
1 Tbsp (15 mL) chopped fresh thyme
1 Tbsp (15 mL) unsalted butter
2 Tbsp (30 mL) brandy
salt and pepper

Preheat a large skillet on the stove.

Add the canola oil to the skillet and sauté the mushrooms until brown. Add the green onion, garlic, parsley, thyme and butter and sauté for 1 minute. Add the brandy and flambé. Season to taste with salt and pepper.

Serve immediately.

---

tip

Oishi Sauce is a PEI-*made sweet soy sauce used for marinades, stir-fries and glazes. It is made from a 100-year-old Japanese family recipe and is available in various stores in Atlantic Canada. A high-quality soy sauce can be substituted in this recipe if necessary.*

potatoes

getting your hands dirty

Prince Edward Island is known the world over for its high-quality table and seed potatoes. As soon as the soil is dry, the Island begins to change colour. The earth that was covered with snow all winter and emerged lifeless in the spring gets ploughed and turned over until it is bright red again, ready for planting seed. Soon after, row after row of potato mounds fill the early summer landscape. Island farmers tend their crop all summer while the rest of us wait for our first taste of the year's new potatoes. Some like them simply boiled and topped with just a little salt, cracked pepper and lots of Island butter. Others prefer to dress them with sour cream, chives, bacon or local cheddar. And there are hundreds of other ways to prepare PEI's original superstar, with new Island traditions being constantly created by home cooks and chefs. PEI potatoes are the anchor for our Island cuisine.

One of my favourite moments in early summer is when the roadside vegetable stands begin to pop up. One of the most important relationships a chef can have is with the farmers who produce the ingredients with which the chef works his or her magic. If you really want to know where to get the best ingredients, look in a chef's refrigerator or pantry in his or her home and find out where these ingredients were sourced.

If you look in my pantry, you will find potatoes from the Lewis family farm in Marshfield. Chad Lewis has worked on the family farm since he was a boy, learning all the tricks of the trade. His father was a farmer, his uncles were farmers and his grandfathers were farmers. There was no doubt that Chad would spend his life tending the land. At a time when small family farms were being sold off to large corporate-run farming operations, Chad chose not to sell his portion of earth but instead to change how he grew, marketed and sold his vegetables.

A trip to his farm is a unique experience. Upon arrival you are greeted with a roadside stand that is bursting at the seams with potatoes and vegetables of all descriptions. You won't find a sales clerk or cash register anywhere; the honour system still operates here (i.e., you select what you want and deposit the exact change into the tin box).

If you are lucky and early enough to find the family in the field, you will see Chad and his wife, Lori-Anne, along with all five of their kids harvesting potatoes. The potatoes are dug one row at a time and are picked by hand and taken to the stand right away. They only pick what they intend to sell that day. If you spend any time with this family you will see a connection to the land and a connection to each other that have somehow been lost on bigger farms that deal in mass volumes of product. Here, everyone contributes to the success of the farm, and they all share the rewards. These are the people I want to work with as a chef. If you can find people who care for the food as much you do, you have a recipe for success.

My trips to this farm always leave me remembering when I experienced long days harvesting potatoes, as a teenager working on Murray Hill Farm with my best bud, Scott. We would sit on the digger or pick rocks from early morning until late at night every day during the fall until the crop was in. At 5 o'clock sharp every day, Elsie Murray, Scott's mother, would show up with the evening meal (one of my fondest memories). There was no time to stop and go home for supper, so supper came to us. This was the one time of year when even the farmhands ate like kings. We had something different every night, including shepherd's pie, stew, or biscuit and potato soup—always hot and always containing potatoes. These are still some of my favourite comfort foods, and, as a chef, I often find myself going back to one version or another of one of these dishes.

Potatoes represent Prince Edward Island's single largest
agricultural commodity in terms of farm cash receipts.
In 2008 Island potato producers harvested 92,500 acres of
potatoes. The farm value of the potato crop can fluctuate
wildly. In the last five years, for example, values have ranged
between $150 million and $205 million, and production was
almost consistently 24.5 million hundredweight (2.45 billion
pounds/1.1 billion kg). About half of the crop is processed
into potato chips and frozen potato products,
and a substantial proportion is shipped out as fresh produce
to eastern Canada, the U.S. and overseas.

yukon gold potato and bacon soup

*This soup recipe is one of those standby favourites that
are perfect on a cold fall night like the ones during
digging season. The most important ingredient is the
potato, but a close second is the people you will share it
with.* SERVES 8

3 Tbsp (45 mL) unsalted butter (softened)
½ lb (250 g) diced bacon
1 cup (250 mL) chopped onion
½ cup (125 mL) chopped carrots
½ cup (125 mL) chopped celery
5 cups (1.25 L) peeled, diced Yukon Gold
  potatoes
8 cups (2 L) chicken stock (page 243)
½ tsp (2 mL) dried sage
1 cup (250 mL) grated cheddar
1 cup (250 mL) whipping cream (or plain
  yogurt or full-fat sour cream)
salt and pepper

Heat the butter in a large saucepan and add the
bacon. Cook the bacon over medium heat until it is
about half-cooked. Add the onion, carrots and celery
and cook for about 5 minutes. Add the potatoes and
chicken stock and bring to a boil. Reduce the heat,
add the sage and simmer, covered, until the potatoes
are tender, 10 to 15 minutes.

Pour the contents into a large blender and
purée (this can be done in batches if your blender
is small). Return the soup to the pot and stir in the
cheese and cream. Season to taste with salt and pepper. The soup can be thinned with some water or
stock if it is too thick.

Serve in large bowls garnished with some sour
cream and chives. Fresh country rolls and sweet tea
finish this soup perfectly.

Chefs get their inspiration from any number of sources, but most will tell you that at some point someone close to them shared a love for food with them and helped cultivate it into something bigger. One of the most powerful food influences in my life was my stepfather, Roger. He was French, straight-from-France French! He loved food and, most importantly, the people who produced the ingredients, and he loved sharing his knowledge. When I was growing up, he and my mom lived in Quebec, and I would visit them on holidays—Christmas, Thanksgiving and every summer. Little did I know that over the years these visits would become mini culinary adventures that would help shape my philosophy as a chef. Roger taught me many things over the years, but it all started with the humble potato. In our home we would prepare a dish called *aligot*, which was a whipped potato dish flavoured with garlic, white wine and cheese. This dish, which originates from Auvergne in central France, introduced me to the simple idea of adding flavours to mashed potatoes.

The flavours you choose are limited only by your imagination, but you must remember that first, you should always start with a perfect mashed potato, and second, always consider what you will be serving the potatoes with. If the flavours don't fit the rest of the meal, you shouldn't use them. We usually served aligot with roast lamb, horse or beef. Of course, there's nothing wrong with having just a big bowl of mashed potatoes for dinner—that way you can go hog-wild in the flavour department!

perfect PEI mashed potatoes eight ways

I have provided the perfect mashed potato recipe, plus some of my favourite flavour combinations. SERVES 8

**3 lb (1.5 kg) mashing potatoes
   (peeled, medium dice)**
**1 cup (250 mL) whipping cream
   or milk (hot)**
⅓ lb (170 g) salted butter (softened)
1½ tsp (7.5 mL) salt
1 tsp (5 mL) freshly ground black pepper

Cover the potatoes in cold water (always cold water) and bring to a boil. Reduce the heat and simmer until a fork slides cleanly through the potato (about 20 minutes). Drain potatoes completely and return to the pot. Add the cream and butter and mash until smooth. Season with the salt and pepper.

=== tips ===

· *Potatoes can take a lot of salt, so season them in stages. Acidic ingredients such as lemon, lime or vinegar can act a bit like salt, so adjust the salt accordingly. Also, not all potatoes are created equal. For this recipe make sure you ask your grocer what would work best as "mashing potatoes."*
· *Potatoes started in cold water cook more consistently than potatoes cooked from boiling water, and the starch doesn't make the finished dish sticky or pasty.*

options:

> BUTTERMILK AND CHIVES: Replace the cream with warm or room-temperature buttermilk and add ½ cup (125 mL) chopped chives at the very end of cooking.

> BACON AND CHEDDAR: Reduce the cream by half and add 1½ cups (375 mL) shredded ADL white cheddar, 1 cup (250 mL) chopped cooked bacon and 1 cup (250 mL) sour cream (full-fat or low-fat, whichever you prefer).

> CILANTRO AND LIME: Reduce the cream by half and add ¼ cup (60 mL) lime juice and ½ cup (125 mL) chopped fresh cilantro.

> ROASTED GARLIC: Add ½ cup (125 mL) roasted garlic purée.

> PARMESAN AND HERB: Add 1 cup (250 mL) freshly grated Parmesan cheese and ½ cup (125 mL) of your favourite chopped fresh herbs.

> LOBSTER AND LEMON: Reduce the salt by one-third. Add 1½ lb (750 g) lobster meat (with its juice), juice of 1 lemon and 1 Tbsp (15 mL) white vinegar.

> BLUE CHEESE: Reduce the salt by one-third. Crumble in 1 cup (250 mL) of your favourite blue cheese—Danish, roquefort, Gorgonzola or Stilton.

> ROASTED CORN AND CHILI: In a medium-sized skillet add 3 Tbsp (45 mL) butter and 1 cup (250 mL) fresh corn niblets (cut from the cob). Sauté until golden brown, then add to the mashed potato with 1 tsp (5 mL) chili powder and a handful of freshly chopped cilantro.

rapure

This is another Acadian specialty that you will find in many homes on PEI. It uses potatoes, which were always plentiful, as well as any leftover meat that need to be used up. It is traditionally served with molasses. This dish gets its name from the French word râper, *which means "to grate." The most traditional recipes feature layers of meat and potatoes, but this one is a bit simpler and quicker to make.* SERVES 8–10

2 onions (small dice)
butter for frying
18 raw potatoes (use mashing potatoes, peeled and grated)
2 cups (500 mL) cooked and mashed potatoes (use mashing potatoes)
1 lb (500 g) cooked meat (pork, chicken or ham) (cut in small pieces)
2 eggs

1 Tbsp (15 mL) chopped fresh summer savory
1 Tbsp (15 mL) baking powder
salt and pepper

Preheat the oven to 350°F (180°C). Grease a deep 9- × 13-inch (3.5 L) casserole dish.

Fry the onions in the butter until tender, about 3 minutes.

Strain the grated potatoes through a fine-mesh sieve lined with cheesecloth to drain all the water.

Mix the raw and cooked potatoes and onion with all the other ingredients and transfer to the prepared casserole dish.

Bake for 2 to 3 hours, or until golden brown.

roasted red pepper potato salad

Nothing says summer like cold potato salad. This recipe has all the classic ingredients with a couple more just to keep it interesting. The roasted red pepper gives a slight pink colour to the salad and unbeliev-able flavour—slightly charred with a little sweetness. —*A.W.* SERVES 8

2 lb (1 kg) potatoes (Yukon Gold preferred)
1 red bell pepper
1¼ cups (310 mL) mayonnaise
4 hard-boiled eggs (chopped)
¼ cup (60 mL) diced celery
¼ cup (60 mL) sliced green onions
¼ cup (60 mL) diced dill pickles
2 Tbsp (30 mL) Dijon mustard
2 Tbsp (30 mL) chopped basil
2 Tbsp (30 mL) chopped fresh parsley
2 tsp (10 mL) hot sauce
salt and pepper

The best way to cook potatoes for potato salad is to wash and boil them whole with the skin on in salted water. Once they are cooked but still a little firm, drain them and allow to cool. Peel them and dice into ½-inch (1 cm) cubes.

To roast the red pepper, place the whole washed red pepper on a preheated barbecue at medium heat and cook, turning occasionally, until the skin blisters and turns black. I know that it sounds a little crazy, but trust me, you will love it. Once all the skin is blistered, remove the pepper from the barbecue, place it in a bowl and cover with plastic wrap for about 10 minutes. This will allow the pepper to steam and become tender. Remove the stem, seeds and blackened skin. It helps if you do this under cold running water. You should be left with the soft cooked flesh of the pepper. Purée the pepper in a food processor.

Mix the potatoes and puréed pepper with all the other ingredients, except the salt and pepper, until well combined. Season to taste with salt and pepper. Refrigerate until ready to serve. For best results refrigerate for at least 1 hour before serving. This will keep for up to 3 days if refrigerated.

chocolate potato cake with red raspberry mud puddles

Potatoes aren't just for a main course or side dish. If you are creative you can find ways to use them for dessert. When I was young, the old woman across the road, Mrs. Foster, would make the most amazing chocolate cake and brownies you could imagine. When we got off the school bus, my brother and I would head straight to her porch, where she had cake and cold milk waiting for us. On a number of Saturday mornings I was lucky enough to make a potato-based cake with her. She told me that the potatoes made the cake super-moist and really dense. I think she was just trying to use up last night's potatoes, but she was right.

This cake is delicious with raspberry sauce, which she would call "raspberry mud puddles." I am not sure where I found this recipe—I like to believe it is hers—but it lives in my kitchen box and is pulled out a few times a year. Potatoes in chocolate cake! Who would've thought? SERVES 6–8

CAKE

1 cup (250 mL) warm Yukon Gold mashed
   potatoes (no salt and passed through
   a food mill or sieve)
1 cup (250 mL) lukewarm water
2 cups (500 mL) all-purpose flour (sifted)
¾ cup (185 mL) unsweetened Dutch-
   processed cocoa powder
2¼ tsp (11 mL) baking powder
2 tsp (10 mL) instant coffee granules
½ tsp (2 mL) baking soda
½ tsp (2 mL) salt
⅔ cup (160 mL) unsalted butter (softened)
2 cups (500 mL) sugar
1 Tbsp (15 mL) vanilla extract
4 eggs
icing sugar

RASPBERRY MUD PUDDLES

2 cups (500 mL) fresh or frozen
   (do not thaw) raspberries
½ cup (125 mL) sugar
¼ cup (60 mL) honey
1 Tbsp (15 mL) lemon juice

continued . . .

CHOCOLATE POTATO CAKE WITH RED RASPBERRY MUD PUDDLES *continued*

Preheat the oven to 350°F (180°C). Spray a deep 9- × 13-inch (3.5 L) baking pan or a 9-inch (23 cm) round cake pan with cooking spray, or grease and flour.

For the cake, place the mashed potatoes in a medium-sized bowl and gradually whisk in the water to form a smooth mixture. You may not need all the water. Do not overmix. Let cool to room temperature.

Sift together the flour, cocoa powder, baking powder, coffee granules, baking soda and salt. Set aside.

Using the paddle attachment of a mixer, combine the butter, sugar and vanilla. Beat at a low speed to blend, and then beat for 1 minute at medium speed, scraping down the bowl and paddle with a rubber spatula once or twice. Add the eggs one at a time, beating in at a low speed after each addition until blended. Scrape down the bowl and paddle with a rubber spatula again. Increase the mixer speed to medium and beat for 1 more minute.

Using the lowest speed, add the sifted dry ingredients in 3 additions and the mashed potato-water mixture in 2 additions, beginning and ending with the dry ingredients, beating just until blended

after each addition. Scrape down the bowl and paddle occasionally with a rubber spatula. Turn the batter into the prepared pan. Spread it level, making sure the batter is pushed right into the corners, then run the batter slightly higher along the pan edges and in the corners.

Bake on the centre rack of the oven for about 30 minutes. The cake is done when a toothpick inserted near the centre emerges with a few moist crumbs still clinging to it. Do not overbake! Remove to a cooling rack, let cool in the pan for 5 to 6 minutes then turn out to cool completely.

For the mud puddles, combine all the ingredients in a small saucepan and mix well. Bring the mixture to a boil, then reduce the heat and simmer for about 5 minutes, stirring occasionally. The sauce is finished cooking when it has a smooth, viscous texture. Remove from the heat and strain out the seeds through a small sieve. Set aside to cool.

To serve, sprinkle icing sugar over the entire surface of the cake. Cut the cake into the desired shape and size. Using a large spoon, form pools of raspberry sauce on large dinner plates. Place a piece of cake on each plate and garnish with a few fresh raspberries.

cheese

from the farm, aged to perfection

When the first settlers came to our Island shores all those years ago, they brought many traditional foods with them, including the cheeses of the Old World. Luckily for us, they also brought the methods and recipes for making those cheeses.

Prince Edward Island is now home to a number of artisan cheesemakers who create award-winning cheddars, flavoured Gouda and many other cheeses that fill the tables of homes and restaurants with true Island flavours. They rely on high-quality milk from dairy cattle across the Island and stick to the tried-and-true traditional methods to produce cheeses that are second to none. Many traditional Island dishes incorporate these cheeses, sometimes as the main ingredient.

Cheese is pretty much front and centre in my home. If you were to open my refrigerator you would find a dozen types at any given time, and they all make their way to the dinner table. I *love* cooking with cheese, and I've found recipes over the years that would be nothing without it. I was born in a small town in England where cheddar is the cheese that shines. When I was very young, my parents and

I came to Canada, but good cheddar was still a staple ingredient in our kitchen, my father very particular about what he'd purchase. We used to get our cheddar from Wendell Mackenzie's little store up the road from where we lived. Wendell still owns that store, and when I go home in summer, I always go there. Wendell is that small-town guy who ends up taking care of all the neighbourhood kids. If one of us had missed the school bus or needed a safe spot until our parents got home, we would hang out on the steps of his shop. Often a slice of cheese and a cold grape-flavoured cola would tide us over until we were picked up.

Wendell stored great blocks of cheddar in his refrigerator and would sell it by weight. It was the good kind of cheddar, aged long enough that it crumbled a bit when he cut it. That cheese formed the foundation of a million omelettes, biscuits, tuna casseroles and scalloped potatoes in the Clement household during my childhood. It was here that I formed my love affair with cheese, and even though I've enjoyed hundreds of different kinds of cheese, that cheddar remains one of my favourites.

ADL Dairy (Amalgamated Dairies Limited) represents all things wholesome when it comes to dairy products. They produce a wide variety of dairy products, everything from chocolate milk to ice cream—but it's their cheese that they're best known for. They make about 10 kinds of cheese, including feta, brick, Colby, mozzarella and havarti, my favourite being their two-year-old white cheddar. It has great flavour and the crumbling qualities I like, plus a nice salty finish. ADL was formed in the 1950s when a number of local dairies facing difficult times were amalgamated. It operates much like a co-op, which means that its members take a special pride of ownership in all they produce. The farmers who supply the milk are all local and have a stake in the end product. They have a real sense of satisfaction in sharing their products with Island communities.

ADL old cheddar gnocchi with chanterelles, peas and basil

Gnocchi is an Italian classic but fits perfectly with Island thinking. You can picture all the ingredients growing around here. I use Prince Edward Island russet potatoes because they are very dry, which is important when making the dough. The ADL old cheddar is an important ingredient because it has a bold, sharp flavour that won't get lost in the potato starch. It's crucial to keep the finished dough warm when you're working with it. As it cools it becomes more difficult to form into shapes and cook properly. If you get it right you will have perfectly cheesy potato dumplings.

SERVES 6—8

3½ lb (1.75 kg) russet potatoes
1 cup (250 mL) grated ADL old white cheddar
2½ cups (625 mL) all-purpose flour
2 eggs
pinch salt
3 Tbsp (45 mL) salted butter
1 lb (500 g) chanterelle mushrooms
½ cup (125 mL) dry white wine
½ lb (250 g) green peas
pinch freshly ground black pepper
1 bunch fresh basil (roughly chopped)
½ cup (125 mL) 2% milk
1 cup (250 mL) ADL whipping cream

Preheat the oven to 400°F (200°C).

Prick the potatoes with a fork, place them on a baking pan and bake until done, about 45 minutes. Turn off the oven. Break the potatoes in half and return them to the oven to dry for an additional half hour. Remove from the oven, peel and pass through a food mill or ricer, or simply mash. Transfer the mash onto a clean pasta board.

Prepare a bowl of ice water. Prepare a large pot of boiling water.

Make a well in the centre of the potatoes and cover completely with all the cheese and flour. Place the eggs and salt in the well and, using a fork, stir them into the flour and potatoes. Once the egg is mixed in, bring the dough together, kneading gently until a ball is formed. Knead gently for a couple of minutes until the ball is dry to the touch. Divide the ball into 4 and roll each one into ¾-inch-diameter (2 cm) dowels. Cut these dowels into 1-inch-long (2.5 cm) pieces. Roll the pieces along the back of a fork or cheese grater to mark them. Drop the pieces into boiling water and cook until they float, 2 to 3 minutes. Transfer to the ice water to cool.

Remove the gnocchi from the water and pat dry. Heat a large skillet or heavy-bottomed saucepan over medium heat. Add the butter then sauté the gnocchi and mushrooms until the gnocchi is slightly crispy and the mushrooms are soft. Deglaze the pan with the white wine and scrape all the tasty bits from the bottom of the pan. Add the peas, pepper, basil, milk and cream, bring to a boil and then reduce to a simmer, stirring occasionally until the cream has reduced to a sauce consistency. Adjust the seasoning with salt, top with more cheddar if you wish just before serving and enjoy with a full-bodied red wine.

Avonlea Clothbound Cheddar made by Cows Creamery is the newest cheese on the Island's food scene. This cheddar is smashing and works perfectly with foods that are smoky and sweet. When you walk into the room where it sits and ages for over a year, it smells like a combination of antique wood and gin. That aroma is very noticeable in the rind of the cheese and slowly fades away as you move closer to the centre. The secret to this cheese's unique flavour is in the cloth wrapping. As the cheddar ages, it is turned regularly to ensure even ripening, and much of the moisture is trapped in the cloth. This moisture gives the rind its flavour and adds to the strength of the cheese.

cows creamery grilled cheese and smoked bacon sandwich

Who doesn't love a grilled cheese sandwich? This is my own variation that includes some of Kenny Mutch's double-smoked bacon from Riverview Market. The superstar in this recipe is definitely the cheddar cheese (you can read more about it on page 204), but its real secret is my father-in-law's homemade apple jelly. He won't give up that recipe, but any homemade apple jelly (we have a recipe on page 115) should work fine. I like this sandwich on a cold fall day with a bowl of roasted tomato soup. SERVES 8

16 slices oatmeal bread

1 cup (250 mL) unsalted butter (softened)

1 cup (250 mL) apple jelly

2 lb (1 kg) Cows Creamery cloth-aged cheddar or your favourite aged cheddar (grated)

1½ lb (750 g) smoked bacon (cooked in whole slices, kept warm)

Generously coat each slice of bread in butter. Turn all the slices over so that the dry side is facing up. Cover this side with a generous layer of apple jelly. Cover every second slice with a layer of grated cheddar. Place 6 slices of bacon on the cheddar and follow with another layer of cheese. Place the remaining jelly-coated slices jelly side down on top of the cheese. There should be 8 complete sandwiches with butter on both the outsides.

Heat a panini grill, place each sandwich on the grill and close the lid. Cook for about 6 minutes until the outside is crisp and golden and the cheese is melted all the way through. If you don't have a panini grill, you can use a griddle or skillet, but you'll have to carefully turn the sandwich over halfway through cooking.

Chefs love to visit the farms where our food comes from. One of my most favourite places to visit is the "Cheese Lady's" place in Winsloe. When you walk into the room, you are greeted by the slightly sour aroma of a cheese room mixed with heaps of herbs and spices. I immediately feel welcome, and I never leave empty-handed. Martina Terbeek is the archetypal Dutch woman with her big smile and no-nonsense warm demeanour. She is a talented cheesemaker who is always willing to give a tour and share the cheesemaking craft. During my last visit, she took me out to the barn where the cows were being milked for the day's cheesemaking. It is always refreshing to spend time with someone who loves what she does. In a way, she is just like a chef. She is creating something she loves and sharing it with whoever is interested. She'll tell you that she is sort of retired, so you never know which days she is going to make her cheese. She makes a number of flavoured varieties of Gouda, but I still prefer the plain one. It is just sharp enough and has a smooth, subtle finish. I bet I've eaten a hundred pounds of her cheese over the years—and I won't be stopping anytime soon.

gouda custard with apple walnut bread and caramel apple gastrique

This is perfect with a cup of coffee or some warm cider. The walnut bread is best when still slightly warm and the custard is light and cheesy. At first, the custard seems almost not sweet enough on its own, but it's balanced out by the sugary gastrique. Serve this to friends on a wintry Saturday morning when you have no reason to go out and just feel like hanging around the house. SERVES 4

GOUDA CUSTARD

⅔ cup (160 mL) whipping cream
⅔ cup (160 mL) 2% milk
¼ lb (125 g) aged Gouda (grated)
2 eggs
2 egg yolks

APPLE WALNUT BREAD

1 cup (250 mL) unsalted butter (softened)
1 cup (250 mL) sugar
4 eggs
4½ cups (1.125 L) all-purpose flour
1 Tbsp (15 mL) baking powder
1 Tbsp (15 mL) baking soda
pinch salt
2 cups (500 mL) sweetened applesauce
½ cup (125 mL) buttermilk (or 1½ tsp/
   7.5 mL vinegar with milk to make
   ½ cup/125 mL)
1 tsp (5 mL) vanilla extract
1 cup (250 mL) chopped walnuts

CARAMEL APPLE GASTRIQUE

1 cup (250 mL) sugar
1 Tbsp (15 mL) corn syrup
1 cup (250 mL) apple cider
1 Tbsp (15 mL) whiskey

Preheat the oven to 350°F (180°C). Line the bottom of four 2 to 3 fl oz (60 to 90 mL) ramekins with parchment paper. Prepare a bain-marie by filling a 9-inch (23 cm) square pan with hot water when the custard is ready to be baked.

For the Gouda custard, in a small saucepan on medium-high heat, add the cream and milk. Bring the mixture just to a boil. Remove from the heat. Whisk in the grated cheese then let cool.

Beat together the eggs and yolks. Temper the egg mixture with some of the warm milk and cheese, then pour the egg mixture into the rest of the milk-cheese mixture. Divide among the prepared ramekins. Bake in the bain-marie on the centre rack of the oven for 25 to 30 minutes, or until the custard is firm when shaken. Let cool on a wire rack and refrigerate until needed.

Increase the oven temperature to 400°F (200°C). Grease a 9- × 5-inch (2 L) loaf pan.

For the walnut bread, using a handheld mixer or blender, cream together the butter and sugar. Break all the eggs into a separate bowl and beat gently; gradually add them to the creamed mixture while continuing to blend.

In a small dish, combine the flour, baking powder, baking soda and salt. In a bowl, combine the applesauce, buttermilk and vanilla. Mix the dry ingredients, alternating with the wet ingredients, into the butter-egg mix. Fold in the walnuts. Pour the batter into the prepared loaf pan. Bake for 20 to 25 minutes or until a toothpick inserted in the centre of the cake comes out clean. Cool in the pan for 5 minutes, then turn out onto a wire rack. Slice when slightly cool.

Meanwhile, make the caramel apple gastrique. In a small saucepan, combine the sugar and corn syrup. Add just enough water to melt the sugar. Increase the heat to high and reduce the mix until the sugar begins to turn golden. Be careful not to let the mixture burn. You shouldn't stir at this stage, but you may want to brush the sides of the pot with water to prevent crystallization. Reduce the heat to medium and carefully add the cider. Again, there is no need to stir at this stage. Continue to reduce until syrupy. Add the whiskey, stirring this time, and cool. You can serve the custard in a nice pool of this nectar, or with this nectar drizzled artfully on the side.

optional:

> You can toss some fresh arugula in a bowl and give it a splash of sherry vinegar, a couple of splashes of extra virgin olive oil, a pinch of sea salt and a few good grinds of fresh ground pepper. Toss with a spoon and add to your plate.

potato bacon cheddar tart

CHEF MICHAEL SMITH, FROM MICHAEL'S *Best of Chef at Home* (WHITECAP BOOKS, 2009)

I've been making this dish for a long time. It's a bit involved, but it remains one of the most impressive potato dishes I know. This special occasion treat features the classic trio of potatoes, bacon and cheddar. It takes some time to make, but the results are more than worth it. It's the sort of thing that looks complicated until you try it and quickly realize how simple it is to master. SERVES 8

> 2 lb (1 kg) bacon
> sea salt and pepper
> 4 cups (1 L) grated aged cheddar
> 6 medium baking potatoes (unpeeled)
> 1 medium onion (small dice)
> 4 cloves garlic (minced)

Preheat the oven to 350°F (180°C).

Carefully arrange the bacon in a radial pattern from the centre of the bottom of a 10- or 12-inch (25 or 30 cm) round non-stick baking pan to the lower edge of the rim and continuing up and over the sides of it. Let the ends hang over. The slices should overlap slightly around the sides of the pan. To reduce the thickness of the bacon in the centre, stagger every other piece. Flatten the centre area, leaving no gaps in the bacon. Season the bacon with lots of pepper and sprinkle on several spoonfuls of the grated cheddar.

Slice the potatoes as thinly and uniformly as you can, about ¼ inch (6 mm) thick (see tip). Arrange a circular pattern of overlapping slices around the inside bottom edge of the pan. Continue arranging overlapping layers of the potatoes until the bottom is evenly covered. Season the potatoes with salt and pepper. Mix together the onion and garlic and sprinkle some of the mixture onto the potatoes. Continue with a layer of the shredded cheese. Cover with another layer of the potato, pressing it down firmly before continuing with alternating layers of the potatoes, onion mixture and cheese, insetting each a bit from the edge of the pan until the top is 1 inch (2.5 cm) or so higher than the pan's rim. Fold the overhanging bacon neatly up and over the top of the potatoes.

Trim a small piece of parchment paper and place it on top of the bacon. Top this with an ovenproof lid. This will prevent the bacon ends from pulling back and shrinking during cooking.

Place the pan on a baking sheet and bake for 2½ to 3 hours. Prick the potatoes with a knife to check that they are cooked through. Pour off as much of the fat around the edges as possible. Let the tart stand for 15 minutes and then invert it onto a cutting surface. Slice into wedges and serve immediately.

optional:

> Try mixing a few spoonfuls of assorted fresh herbs into the onion mixture. Thyme, rosemary and tarragon all work well.

---

tip

Kitchen specialty stores carry a French slicing tool known as a mandoline. It's a fancy chef tool and easily slices the potatoes into even rounds. It's not absolutely necessary, though— a sharp knife works well, too!

---

baked brie with berries in filo pastry

This is one for your next party. Your guests are sure to adore the richness of the cheese balanced by the tartness of the berries along with the crunch of the pastry.

SERVES 4—6

2 sheets filo pastry
3 Tbsp (45 mL) salted butter (melted)
1 small wheel brie (½ lb/250 g)
¼ cup (60 mL) mixed berries (strawberries,
    blackberries, raspberries, blueberries)
    (if using frozen, thaw and drain off liquid
    before using)
2 Tbsp (30 mL) sliced toasted almonds

Preheat the oven to 375°F (190°C). Butter a baking sheet.

Lay 1 sheet of filo on a clean work surface and brush it with melted butter. Place the other sheet on top and brush it with butter. Place the brie in the centre, place the berries on top and sprinkle with the toasted almonds.

Bring the 4 corners of the pastry together and pinch closed just above the cheese, berries and almonds. Place on the prepared baking sheet and bake for 8 to 10 minutes, or until golden brown.

Serve immediately.

wine & spirits

an age-old tradition

Prince Edward Island has a rich history of producing and promoting artisanal alcoholic drinks. In the age of Prohibition, rum-runners would ply their trade in the vast waters surrounding the Island. These days we have John Rossignol of Rossignol Estate Winery in Little Sands, on the southeastern shore. John is an award-winning winemaker, specializing in fruit wines—apple, cranberry, strawberry-rhubarb, blueberry, blackberry and, of course, grapes. John uses as much locally sourced fruit as he can get his hands on. We also have Myriad View Artisan Distillery in eastern PEI, which produces PEI shine, the only legal moonshine (now there's a contradiction in terms!) you'll ever have the chance to buy. They also produce vodka and gin. And Prince Edward Distillery, also in eastern PEI, specializes in vodka production.

Local wine, beer and spirits are almost as important to a chef as local food. Places like France, Italy and Portugal have a long and distinguished history of producing some of the finest wines and spirits in the world. Prince Edward Island has recently taken steps to emulate these culinary role models by dramatically increasing the amount of locally produced fruit wine, spirits and beer. Rossignol Winery led the charge.

In 1990 John Rossignol left Ontario to build a house in Little Sands, Prince Edward Island. At first John wasn't sure what direction he wanted his career to take. While he pondered, he began making his own wine. Winemaking brought out his creative side, and he found himself experimenting with different methods, as well as creating new mixtures of grapes and other fruit and turning them into wonderful wine. John's fun hobby eventually led to the creation of the first commercial winery on the Island: Rossignol Winery. In 1994 he added more plants, and that summer he saw his first product, non-grape wines from frozen fruit harvested the previous year, while he waited for his licence to come through. And that fall he bottled his first grape table wines.

In light of the winery's impressive success at several prestigious competitions, John is now looking at marketing his wines across Canada. While many Island businesses export their products, John had encountered several unexpected legal obstacles, "regulations that were left over from the Prohibition days," he says. Fortunately, the regulations were

recently revised, allowing Rossignol wines to be shipped directly off-Island.

Rossignol Winery shuns pesticides and operates as an ecologically friendly vineyard in strip-crop fashion. The grapes are grown with ample green space between the rows, and the nearby Northumberland Strait guarantees that a fresh breeze is never too far away. These two things help the vineyard to stay fungus free. And John Rossignol continues to push the winemaking envelope. The Island's now-defunct tobacco-growing industry has resulted in an abundance of unused greenhouses. John seized on this opportunity and started using the buildings to grow the more fragile grapes. With about a hectare of grapes too tender to normally be grown on the Island, John has been able to produce Cabernet Franc, Merlot and Chardonnay varieties. Although highly untraditional—and quite possibly the only greenhouse grapes grown in Canada—the products are a success, as the wines have come to taste clean and traditional.

Rossignol Winery uses only pure oak barrels, rather than oak chip or oak seasonings. This adds a traditional flavour to the premium reds, as well as a unique flavour to Rossignol's Haneveldt Apple Cider. John testifies that oak barrels do make a difference. With traditional barrel aging, some of the moisture evaporates through the porous wood, intensifying the fruit and at the same time giving it the oak flavour.

Aside from the grape wines, the fruit wines are also part of the Rossignol Winery's successes. "Fruit wines are really the true regional product for the Maritimes and Eastern Seaboard. So we are trying to raise the profile of fruit wines by winning medals with both fruit and table wines, just to establish in the eye of the consumer that the fruit wines are a quality item," says John.

warm ginger cake with a liberty blossom reduction

This recipe is a traditional favourite. We've paired this spiced warm cake with a reduction of Rossignol Estate Winery's Iced Liberty Blossom Wine—made from apple juice that is frozen and has some of the water removed, leaving concentrated apple nectar that is fermented and finished to a crisp, sweet intense apple wine. Old Towne Orchard and Marc Brunet of Warburton Road supplies Rossignol with some of his apples for his apple wine. SERVES 8

LIBERTY BLOSSOM REDUCTION
3 cups (750 mL) Rossignol Liberty
   Blossom Wine
1 cup (250 mL) sugar
3 Tbsp (45 mL) honey

CAKE
½ cup (125 mL) unsalted butter (softened)
¼ cup (60 mL) golden corn syrup
½ cup (125 mL) dark brown sugar (packed)
1 cup (250 mL) all-purpose flour
2 tsp (10 mL) baking powder
1 tsp (5 mL) ground ginger
2 Tbsp (30 mL) finely grated fresh ginger
1 egg
2 Tbsp (30 mL) 2% milk

For the reduction, combine the wine, sugar and honey in a saucepan. Slowly bring to a boil, making sure the sugar and honey are dissolved. Reduce the heat to medium and simmer until one-third of the liquid remains. Remove from the heat and let cool.

Preheat the oven to 350°F (180°C). Lightly grease a 9- × 5-inch (2 L) loaf pan or a deep 6-inch (15 mL) round cake tin with butter or oil.

For the cake, melt the butter, syrup and sugar in a saucepan over low heat. Give it a thorough stir to mix well. Let cool for 2 to 3 minutes.

Meanwhile, mix the flour, baking powder and ground ginger in a mixing bowl. Add the fresh ginger, mixing it evenly throughout the flour mixture.

Beat the egg and milk together slowly and stir into the butter-syrup mixture in the saucepan. Ensure that the syrup is not too hot, or the egg will curdle. Pour this into the dry ingredients. Gently fold all the ingredients in until the flour is completely moistened. Avoid overmixing. Transfer the mixture to the prepared pan.

Bake in the centre of the oven for about 40 minutes, or until well risen and coming away slightly from the sides. Insert a toothpick into the centre of the cake to see if it comes out clean. Turn the cake out of the pan and cool on a wire rack. Serve a couple of slices of this cake with a drizzle of the Liberty Blossom reduction. You could also serve a shot glass of the reduction so that you can dip the cake into it.

Rossignol Estate Winery has won its fair share of national awards. They produce blueberry wine, strawberry wine, strawberry-rhubarb wine, cranberry wine, Raspberry Festival (a nice wine for dessert or a special brunch), blackberry mead, Liberty Blossom iced apple wine and Isle St. Jean red and white wine (made from grapes, of course). All the winery's wine labels are replicas of original Island artwork painted by John Rossignol and his wife, Dagny, as well as neighbour and Island folk artist Nancy Perkins. The terroir of the Little Sands winery makes it a beautiful destination all on its own—experiencing the wine and witnessing John's passion for what he does are the gravy.

PEI *has made strides to establish a legal, local wine and spirit industry. Even brew pubs, like Gahan House Brewery, have come on the scene to offer locals and tourists alike a locally handcrafted, world-class quality beer. As* PEI *entrepreneurs like John Rossignol continue to succeed, they help other people to find their niche on this Island of ours.*

dalvay's sticky date pudding with toffee sauce

No PEI *cookbook would be complete without Dalvay by the Sea's famous recipe. I've added some rum to the toffee sauce as a tribute to* PEI*'s rich history of rum-running back in the days of Prohibition, but you can leave it out if you prefer.* SERVES 6—8

STICKY DATE PUDDING
1¾ cups (435 mL) dates (pitted)
2 cups (500 mL) water
1½ tsp (7.5 mL) baking soda
6 Tbsp (90 mL) unsalted butter (softened)
1 cup (250 mL) sugar
3 eggs
2 cups (500 mL) all-purpose flour
½ tsp (2 mL) baking powder
½ tsp (2 mL) ground ginger
½ tsp (2 mL) salt

TOFFEE SAUCE
¾ cup (185 mL) unsalted butter
1¼ cups (310 mL) brown sugar (packed)
1 cup (250 mL) whipping cream
½ tsp (2 mL) vanilla extract (optional)
1 fl oz (30 mL) dark rum (optional)

Preheat the oven to 375°F (190°C). Line an 8-inch (20 cm) square baking pan with parchment paper. Half-fill a larger baking pan with hot water.

For the pudding, chop the dates coarsely, place them in a small saucepan with the water and bring to a boil for 5 minutes. Remove the saucepan from the heat, mix in the baking soda and let stand for 20 minutes.

In a bowl, cream together the butter and sugar, adding the eggs one by one, mixing well after each addition.

In a separate bowl, sift together the flour, baking powder, ground ginger and salt. Use a spoon to work this into the egg mixture. Finally, add the date mixture and combine all the ingredients well.

Pour the mix into the prepared baking pan and sit the pan in the water bath. Bake for 20 minutes, then reduce the oven temperature to 300°F (150°C) until the cake is cooked, 25 more minutes, or until a toothpick comes out clean when inserted in the middle. Cut in 8 squares.

For the toffee sauce, melt the butter and dissolve the sugar in it over medium heat. Add the cream and, if using, the vanilla and rum. Simmer for 5 minutes until thickened slightly, stirring just to incorporate.

Serve the pudding warm with warm toffee sauce and vanilla ice cream. The pudding can be made ahead and kept refrigerated until needed. It can be reheated by steamer, or lightly microwaved, before serving.

Rum, produced in the West Indies from sugar cane, played a huge part in the history of Prince Edward Island. The legendary rum-runner ship, the *Nellie J. Banks*, that sailed out of Naufrage on the north side, ran a lively trade when anchored off the waters of the Island. It would meet small boats of local men who would purchase or trade moonshine during Prohibition days. Prohibition lasted longer on Prince Edward Island, from 1900 to 1948, than in any other place in North America. The trade was two-sided. Illegal moonshine produced on PEI would be shipped to the United States, to destinations linked to organized crime.

Rum is still a popular option here. I guess some things are just entrenched in our roots—my father's father, his father and his father's father all drank rum. It's part of the culture. In some of the stories passed on in my family, rum was the reason for the ever-popular trip to the barn when company was over. "Harl would have his bottle hid in the sleigh under his seat, and Dad would pull his private stash from some hay-camouflaged nook up in the rafters of the barn, and don't forget the mickey in Uncle Percy's boot. They would all congress out in the barn to 'check on a lame horse' or 'sick cow.'" There seemed to be a lot of sick animals in the barns of rural PEI, back in those days. Prohibition, funnily enough, was a golden era for the local speakeasy, a tradition that still carries on today. Every Island community has its own "local"—a place of the people, with lots of great local music, local characters and great stories. You can wet your whistle any day, anytime—but you have to know a local, have talked in-depth with a local or stalked a local to find these history-rich watering holes. If you happen in by chance, you should embrace the experience. Listen to the stories the locals tell you. You'll not hear anything like them anywhere else in the world.

bloody mary–steamed salmon

CHEF MICHAEL SMITH, FROM MICHAEL'S *Best of Chef at Home* (WHITECAP BOOKS, 2009)

One of the easiest ways to cook any type of fish is to simply simmer it in a flavourful liquid. And if that liquid just happens to taste like a classic cocktail, all the better! This dish tastes like a special occasion, but you can actually put it together in minutes. SERVES 4

four 6 oz (175 g) salmon fillets
salt and pepper
2 cups (500 mL) tomato juice
4 fl oz (125 mL) finest vodka
1 Tbsp (15 mL) horseradish

1 Tbsp (15 mL) Worcestershire sauce
zest and juice of 1 lemon
splash or two of olive oil
2 stalks celery (chopped)

Season the salmon fillets with lots of salt and pepper.

Mix the remaining ingredients in a shallow saucepan with a tight-fitting lid. Bring to a gentle simmer and then add the salmon fillets. Cover, and poach the salmon in the flavourful liquid until just cooked through, about 10 minutes. Serve each fillet in a bowl with the cooking broth ladled overtop.

> ≈ tip ≈
>
> *When you cook, all the flavour molecules dissolve in the cooking water, fat or alcohol. In this dish the vodka highlights an additional layer of flavours in the tomato juice. You may substitute an aromatic gin for a different aromatic flavour. Try filling the serving bowls with a handful of baby spinach before adding the salmon and broth.*

As a chef, I always have a keen interest in checking out local wineries and distilleries whenever my wife and I are travelling. When we were in France, we toured the countryside, visiting many regional wineries as well as cognac and Armagnac distilleries. We visited Portugal to see the port distilleries and wineries along the Douro River, and we've been to wineries and grappa distilleries in Italy. But of all the distilleries, my favourites are the scotch distilleries in Scotland and the whiskey distilleries and breweries in Ireland.

cranberry sangria

This thirst-quencher is a perfect libation at any time of year, whether with a Thanksgiving dinner or a summer picnic in the backyard. Cranberries are grown locally in both the eastern and western ends of the province, and of course PEI cranberries have inspired John Rossignol to make a vibrant cranberry wine.

MAKES 8 CUPS (2 L)

3 cups (750 mL) Rossignol cranberry wine
2 cups (500 mL) cranberry juice
2 cups (500 mL) sparkling mineral water
  or ginger ale (if you prefer sweeter)
1 lime (sliced)
1 lemon (sliced)
½ cup (125 mL) fresh cranberries
ice cubes

Combine all the ingredients in a pitcher with your preferred amount of ice, and stir.

The local chef's association often hosts fundraising dinners to promote local ingredients. This has become the group mission of the Island chef scene. We all appreciate the local suppliers who supply endless amounts of fresh garden produce, and we make sure we pair local ingredients with an evolving menu of locally made wines and spirits. Sometimes John from the Rossignol Estate Winery will supply a bottle from his wine cellar, maybe a Liberty Blossom to match a warm ginger cake or a Raspberry Festival paired with a dark chocolate mousse and fresh-from-the-raspberry-patch raspberry compote.

Other local distilleries also take part as they expand their repertoire. Dinners like these are a great way for distillery owners to promote their product directly by having people try it. Their passion is evident to all who talk to them on these nights; no parent was ever so proud to see his or her "baby" shown off. I recommend Myriad View Artisan Distillery's "Strait Gin" paired with Johnny Flynn's oysters from just down the road. Shoot them separately or together in an oyster martini. Either way you'll be astounded.

The Prince Edward Distillery's PEI Potato Vodka, a pure, crisp premium vodka made from local Island potatoes, craftily distilled in Hermanville (en route to North Lake), is another gem. The women from the distillery are really making a mark for themselves with this high-end smooth-as-silk liquor—especially when the bottle is frozen for that cold, velvet feeling. It is cleverly marketed in a miniature lobster trap, making it truly "Prince Edward Island." They also distill a blueberry-infused vodka made from grain. They even recycle the mash from the fermented tanks and feed it to their herd of little pigs; they then sell the fatted pigs to local restaurants.

Everything comes full circle when we serve that roast pork, fresh off the spit. A crispy, juicy mess of protein goodness. Imagine a generous selection of condiments—sweet mustards, savoury mustards, hot mustards and even hotter mustards, apple and sage chutney, whiskey onion marmalade, horseradish applesauce, rummed-up raisin onion compote; add some crusty bread; and wash it all down with a generous shot of that ice-cold potato vodka. Wow—it doesn't get much better than that. And talk about a pure moment. It's all about local! It's about respect and about getting to know our local champions and helping each other get the word out. It's a symbiotic relationship between the chef and the producer, and the goal is always to create an unforgettable experience for the diner.

essentials

essentials

This section is full of recipes that you'll use over and over again. We've included standard items like stocks and dressings, but we've also thrown in a few of our favourite quick appetizers and baked goods. Some of the recipes like stocks and pie pastry can be frozen so that you always have something good in your kitchen to rely on. Of course fresh is best—there's no way we would argue with that one—but sometimes it's good to keep some pre-made items on hand.

pie pastry

This recipe makes enough pastry for three double crusts. Freeze the unused portions of dough in well-sealed plastic bags for up to two months. It's always good to have some extra pastry on hand—you never know when you will need it. You can use vegetable shortening (Crisco or Tenderflake) in place of the lard if you prefer, but the pastry won't be quite as good. MAKES ENOUGH FOR 3 DOUBLE CRUSTS (DEPENDING ON PIE SIZE)

5½ cups (1.375 L) all-purpose flour
2 tsp (10 mL) sea salt
1 lb (500 g) lard
1 Tbsp (15 mL) white vinegar
1 egg (lightly beaten)
cold water as needed

Mix together the flour and salt. Cut in the lard and mix with your hands or a pastry blender until the flour is coarse and pea-sized.

Combine the vinegar and egg in a 1-cup (250 mL) measure. Add enough cold water to make 1 cup (250 mL). Gradually add this to the flour-lard mixture, being careful to add just enough liquid to bring the dough together.

Divide the dough into 6 equal pieces, wrap with cling film and chill for 1 hour.

Roll out 1 portion of dough onto a lightly floured surface to ¼-inch (6 mm) thickness. Transfer the rolled dough to a pie plate dampened with water (size according to your recipe), and trim the edges of the pastry.

Roll out a second portion of dough and reserve for a top crust.

Freeze any unused portions of dough.

tart dough

This is a versatile general tart dough that is quick and easy to make. Try it with the cranberry curd (page 143). MAKES ENOUGH FOR ONE 10- TO 12-INCH (25 TO 30 CM) TART

1 cup (250 mL) unsalted butter (softened)
⅓ cup (80 mL) sugar
4 egg yolks
2 cups (500 mL) all-purpose flour
1 tsp (5 mL) sea salt

Cream the butter and sugar together until smooth. Add all the egg yolks and blend until incorporated. Stir in the flour and salt and mix just until the dough comes together.

Turn out onto a lightly floured surface and knead for 1 minute. Shape the dough into a disc, wrap and then chill for at least 1 hour.

The dough should be removed from the refrigerator 1 hour before using.

Preheat the oven to 375°F (190°C).

On a lightly floured surface, knead the dough again for 1 minute. Roll out the pastry to ¼ inch (6 mm) thick.

Line a 10- to 12-inch (25 to 30 cm) tart pan with the dough, trim the rough edges and chill for 30 minutes.

Prick the crust bottom with a fork and blind bake for 15 to 20 minutes, until the edges are lightly browned and the centre of the shell is dry. Allow to cool before filling.

pizza dough

Here is a simple and fast recipe for making your own pizza crust. You can make it in a mixer or knead it by hand if you prefer. MAKES TWO 12-INCH (30 CM) PIZZA CRUSTS

> 1 cup (250 mL) warm water
> 2 Tbsp (30 mL) instant yeast
> 1 Tbsp (15 mL) sugar
> 4 cups (2.2 lb/1 kg) all-purpose flour
> 2 tsp (10 mL) sea salt
> 2 Tbsp (30 mL) virgin olive oil
> cornmeal

In a small bowl place the water, yeast and sugar. Let sit for 5 to 10 minutes to activate the yeast.

Place the flour and salt in the bowl of a mixer with a dough hook attached and turn the mixer on. Slowly add the water-yeast mixture and olive oil while the machine is running. Continue to run the mixer at a low speed until the dough is thoroughly mixed.

Increase the speed to medium for 5 minutes (if making by hand, knead for 10 minutes).

Grease a bowl.

Transfer the dough to the bowl, cover with a towel and let sit in a warm place until doubled in size, about 25 minutes. Punch down the proofed dough then let it bench-rest for 5 minutes. Divide it in half.

Roll out the dough on a well-floured surface to make an 8-inch (20 cm) circle.

Sprinkle some cornmeal over a greased pizza stone or pan and place the dough down gently, pressing it out to cover the entire surface. This recipe makes a thin-crust pizza. If you like a thicker crust, simply roll out the dough to a smaller diameter.

Preheat the oven to 400°F (200°C).

Cover the pizza dough with your favourite toppings and sauces and bake for 20 to 25 minutes.

savoury bread pudding base

This is a versatile recipe that can be made with whatever you have in the refrigerator. I have listed a few of my favourite variations. We have it for brunch at my house!—J.M. SERVES 6–8

> 4 cups (1 L) cubed day-old bread
>   (any bread is fine)
> 6 eggs
> 2 cups (500 mL) whipping cream
> 1 tsp (5 mL) nutmeg
> salt and pepper

Preheat the oven to 350°F (180°C). Spray a 9- × 13-inch (3.5 L) casserole dish with cooking spray.

Place the bread into the prepared dish. In a bowl gently beat together the eggs, cream and seasonings. Pour over the bread cubes and let soak for at least 20 minutes—this is the key!

Bake for 30 minutes or until puffed and golden.

flavour additions:

These tasty extras can be added after the bread has soaked.

> APPLE, CHEDDAR AND BACON. Combine 1 cup (250 mL) chopped apples, 1 cup (250 mL) grated cheddar and ½ cup (125 mL) chopped, cooked bacon.

> HAM, SWISS AND BROCCOLI. Combine 1 cup (250 mL) diced ham, 1 cup (250 mL) grated Swiss cheese and 1 cup (250 mL) steamed broccoli flowerets.

> TOMATO, BASIL AND PROVOLONE. Combine ½ cup (125 mL) diced tomatoes, ¼ cup (60 mL) chopped fresh basil and 1 cup (250 mL) provolone for an Italian twist!

buttermilk biscuits

Few things make you feel more at home than a hot buttermilk biscuit. You can add all kinds of things to them if you like (herbs, cheese, chopped ham—the recipe that follows includes both ham and cheddar), but I still enjoy the plain version. The trick is to avoid kneading the dough too much and to keep the dough a little moist.—A.C. MAKES ABOUT 18 LARGE BISCUITS

3 cups (750 mL) all-purpose flour
1½ Tbsp (22.5 mL) baking powder
1 tsp (5 mL) baking soda
1 tsp (5 mL) sea salt
1 tsp (5 mL) freshly ground black pepper
¾ cup (185 mL) unsalted butter
   (cold, cubed)
¾ cup (185 mL) buttermilk

Preheat the oven to 425°F (220°C), then grease a baking sheet.

In a large bowl, sift together the flour, baking powder, baking soda, salt and pepper. Using your hands, blend in the butter until the mix is about the size of small peas. Make a well in the middle and pour in the buttermilk. Using a fork, gently combine the mix until a loose ball forms.

Transfer the ball to a pastry board and roll out to about ½ inch (1 cm) thick. Cut the dough into rounds with a 2-inch (5 cm) cookie cutter and transfer them to the prepared baking sheet.

Bake for 15 minutes, or until golden.

Enjoy these biscuits by themselves or with a stew or chowder.

ham and cheese biscuits

This recipe is a favourite at my house. It also is a good use for some of that ham leftover from supper the night before. Vary the type of cheese to mix things up—try blue cheese, Parmesan, Gouda or Swiss.—J.M. MAKES 12 BISCUITS

3 cups (750 mL) all-purpose flour
2 Tbsp (30 mL) sugar
1½ Tbsp (22.5 mL) baking powder
1 tsp (5 mL) sea salt
½ lb (250 g) unsalted butter (cold, cubed)
1 cup (250 mL) grated cheddar
1 cup (250 mL) diced ham
1½ cups (375 mL) buttermilk
   (or 1½ Tbsp/22.5 mL vinegar with
   enough milk to make 1½ cups/375 mL)

Preheat the oven to 400°F (200°C). Line a baking sheet with parchment paper, or grease lightly.

Combine the flour, sugar, baking powder and salt. Cut in the butter and mix by hand until the mixture appears crumbly. Add the cheese and ham and mix in with your hands.

Make a well in the centre of the dry mixture and add the buttermilk. Mix with a fork until combined. Do not overmix. On a floured surface, roll out the dough and cut it into the desired shape—circles, triangles, etc. Transfer the biscuits to the prepared baking sheet.

Bake for 15 to 20 minutes, or until slightly golden.

Serve warm with butter.

veggie dip

This a great recipe for dipping your fresh garden veggies and sweet potato fries. MAKES 1 CUP (250 ML)

½ cup (125 mL) mayonnaise
(low-fat if you prefer)
½ cup (125 mL) sour cream
(low-fat if you prefer)
2 Tbsp (30 mL) minced red onion
1 Tbsp (15 mL) chopped fresh dill
1 tsp (5 mL) garlic powder
½ tsp (2 mL) onion powder
dash Tabasco sauce
salt and pepper

Combine all the ingredients, check the seasoning and place in an airtight container until needed.

This is best made a couple hours before needed to let the flavours meld. It keeps refrigerated in an airtight container for up to 1 week.

guacamole

Everyone needs a good guacamole recipe. This one is simple and easy to prepare. And avocados have the added bonus of being a great source of good fat. MAKES 1½–2 CUPS (375–500 ML)

1 ripe avocado
3 Tbsp (45 mL) sour cream (low-fat if you prefer)
3 Tbsp (45 mL) chopped fresh cilantro
3 Tbsp (45 mL) finely diced red and green bell pepper
2 Tbsp (30 mL) crushed garlic
2 Tbsp (30 mL) lime juice
2 tsp (10 mL) hot sauce
salt and pepper

Cut the avocado in half and remove the pit and skin. Place the avocado, sour cream, cilantro, peppers, garlic, lime juice and hot sauce in a food processor and purée until smooth.

Season to taste with salt and pepper. Transfer to a serving dish, cover and chill for 1 hour before serving.

roasted garlic hummus

Most hummus recipes call for tahini, and that is certainly traditional. However, the beauty of cooking is that things don't have to be traditional. Try using 3 Tbsp (45 mL) of cream cheese or 3 Tbsp (45 mL) of roasted red pepper instead, for another dimension in flavour and texture. This recipe is a great starting point that can go in many directions.—A.W. MAKES 3 CUPS (750 ML)

2 cups (500 mL) cooked chickpeas
   (start with ¾ cup if using dried)
6 cloves garlic (peeled)
3 Tbsp (45 mL) extra virgin olive oil
2 Tbsp (30 mL) tahini (sesame seed paste)
3 Tbsp (45 mL) lemon juice
salt and white pepper
2 Tbsp (30 mL) chopped fresh parsley
1 tsp (5 mL) paprika

If you're using dried chickpeas, place in a bowl and cover with cold water. Let sit overnight. Drain the chickpeas and place in a small pot. Cover with hot water, bring to a boil and simmer until the chickpeas are soft and lose their crunch. If you're using canned, simply rinse and drain.

Preheat the oven to 325°F (160°C).

Toss the garlic cloves with 1 Tbsp (15 mL) of the olive oil and roast for 15 to 20 minutes.

Place the chickpeas, roasted garlic, tahini (if using) and the remaining olive oil in a food processor and blend until smooth. Add the lemon juice a little at a time and taste in between additions. I prefer a little more lemon than other people, but that's just me. It should take about 3 Tbsp (45 mL). Season to taste with salt and pepper.

Place the hummus in a serving dish. Drizzle with additional olive oil and sprinkle with chopped parsley and paprika.

Serve with warm pitas.

PEI pickled eggs

Pickled eggs are popular all over Prince Edward Island—they are simple to make and keep for months in the refrigerator. This recipe is the one I make at home. I serve them with meat platters or salads, or as a snack. When I was dating my wife, she introduced me to a canapé that I now use at parties all the time. Simply place a slice of pickled egg on your favourite cracker, put a slice of sweet pickle on the egg and top with a piece of old cheddar. This is an adapted version of the recipe her father used. You know it must be good; I married her!—A.C. MAKES 24 EGGS

5 cups (1.25 L) white vinegar
1 cup (250 mL) water
1 cup (250 mL) sugar
2 cups (500 mL) small-diced onion
5 cloves garlic (minced)
1 bay leaf
1 Tbsp (15 mL) freshly cracked black pepper
1 Tbsp (15 mL) yellow mustard seeds
1 Tbsp (15 mL) coriander seeds
24 hard-boiled eggs (cooled and peeled)

Combine all the ingredients except the eggs in a pot and bring to a boil. Reduce the heat and simmer for 2 minutes. Let cool slightly.

Place the eggs in a sterile 2-quart (2 L) jar and pour the warm vinegar mixture overtop. If the vinegar is hot rather than warm it will turn the egg yolks green.

Cover, cool and refrigerate for at least 1 week before eating. These last forever if they're refrigerated! However, I recommend eating them within 2 to 3 weeks before they become way too strong.

crab cakes

Crab cakes make a great appetizer on their own, especially with some tartar sauce on the side. They can also be used as ingredients in more complex appetizers. Whichever way you look at it, they are delicious!

SERVES 4—6

3 green onions (small dice)

¾ cup (185 mL) vermouth

¼ cup (60 mL) dry white wine

2½ lb (1.25 kg) cooked rock crab (squeeze out excess moisture)

⅓ cup (80 mL) fresh chopped tarragon

1 egg white

⅓ cup (80 mL) grated cooked potato (russet or Yukon Gold work well)

dash Tabasco sauce

1 tsp (5 mL) lemon juice

salt and pepper

½ cup (125 mL) all-purpose flour

2 eggs (beaten)

1 cup (250 mL) instant potato flakes

¼ cup (60 mL) salted butter

Preheat the oven to 350°F (180°C).

In a skillet over low heat, cook the green onions, vermouth and wine until most of the moisture has been evaporated and the green onions are barely damp. Let cool in the pan.

Combine crab, tarragon, egg white, potato, Tabasco sauce and lemon juice. Add green onions and season with salt and pepper. Mix thoroughly.

Using a 2-inch (5 cm) mould, form the mixture into cakes 2 inches (5 cm) high.

Dip each cake in the flour, then the egg and finally the potato flakes.

Heat the butter in an ovenproof pan over medium-high heat. Brown all sides of the cakes, then transfer to the oven for 7 minutes.

Garnish with chopped fresh herbs and serve hot. These are best served immediately.

beef stock

A good beef stock is often the foundation of a great stew, braise or sauce. The rich flavour in this stock comes from roasting the bones and vegetables, then slowly simmering them to extract all the flavours. This recipe is simple, but it produces a robust, beefy, dark-coloured stock. MAKES 4–5 QUARTS (4–5 L)

3 Tbsp (45 mL) vegetable oil
5 lb (2.2 kg) beef bones
12 oz (375 g) medium-diced carrots (peeled)
6 oz (175 g) medium-diced celery
6 oz (175 g) medium-diced onion
5 cloves garlic (peeled and crushed slightly)
3 Tbsp (45 mL) tomato paste
1 cup (250 mL) red wine
3 sprigs fresh parsley
2 sprigs fresh thyme
2 bay leaves
5 quarts (5 L) cold water

Preheat the oven to 400°F (200°C).

In a large roasting pan on the stovetop, heat the oil until hot and brown the bones on all sides. Add the carrots, celery, onion and garlic and brown them slightly. Transfer the pan to the oven for 30 minutes. Turn the bones, cover them with the tomato paste and roast for another 20 minutes.

Remove the bones and vegetables from the roasting pan and deglaze the pan with the red wine, being sure to scrape all the bits from the pan. Place the bones, vegetables and red wine in a stockpot and add the parsley, thyme and bay leaves. Cover the bones with the cold water and bring to a simmer.

Simmer for 6 hours, uncovered, skimming off the impurities that float to the top every 30 minutes. Do not boil the stock or it will become bitter.

Gently remove the bones, vegetables and bay leaves from the stock, then strain it through a fine-mesh sieve or cheesecloth.

Quickly cool the stock and refrigerate for up to 5 days until needed. Pour any unused stock into freezer-safe containers and freeze for up to 3 months.

---

tip

You can buy beef bones as well as chicken bones from your local butcher. If you seal them in a bag, they should keep for up to 3 months in the freezer. You'll need to take the bones out the freezer to thaw the day before you make your stock.

chicken stock

Every cook should know how to make a chicken stock. It is cheap and easy to make and can be the foundation of many soups and sauces. It will also have your home smelling fantastic all afternoon. Remember to use high-quality, fresh ingredients for the best results. The old myth that the stockpot is the kitchen garbage can is just that—a myth. Good chefs know that great results come from great ingredients, and stocks are no exception. MAKES 4–5 QUARTS (4–5 L)

- 5 lb (2.2 kg) fresh chicken bones (necks and backs work best)
- 5 quarts (5 L) cold water
- 8 oz (250 g) carrots (peeled, medium dice)
- 4 oz (125 g) celery (medium dice)
- 4 oz (125 g) onion (medium dice)
- 3 cloves garlic (peeled and crushed slightly)
- 2 bay leaves
- 1 sprig fresh thyme
- 3 sprigs fresh parsley

Rinse the bones well and put them in a 10-quart (10 L) stockpot. Cover them with cold water and bring to a simmer. Remove from the heat, then remove the bones from the pot and transfer them to another stockpot. This step is called blanching, and it gets rid of the unwanted impurities on the bones and ensures a clearer, more flavourful stock. If you skip this step your stock will be cloudy and have a bitter undertone.

Cover the bones with 5 quarts (5 L) of fresh cold water and bring to a simmer.

Add the remaining ingredients and simmer, uncovered, for 4 hours, skimming off the impurities that float to the top every 20 minutes. Do not boil the stock or it will become cloudy.

Gently remove the bones, vegetables and bay leaves from the stock, then strain it through a fine-mesh sieve or cheesecloth.

Quickly cool the stock and refrigerate for up to 5 days until needed. Pour any unused stock into freezer-safe containers and freeze for up to 3 months.

fish stock

A good fish stock can add intense flavour to chowder or fish stew, and the bonus is that it is easy to make. The trick is to choose fish bones that are lean and fresh. Note that you don't use any ingredients that will colour the stock, such as carrots or tomato. The goal is to have a rich, flavourful clear liquid. MAKES ABOUT 5½ QUARTS (5.5 L)

> 5 lb (2.2 kg) lean white fish bones
>   (halibut, haddock or cod)
> ¾ cup (185 mL) small-diced celery
> ¾ cup (185 mL) small-diced onion
> ½ lemon
> 3 sprigs fresh parsley
> 2 sprigs fresh thyme
> 2 bay leaves
> 5 quarts (5 L) cold water

Rinse the bones in cold water and transfer to a 12-quart (12 L) stockpot. (You can blanch them if you would prefer a very clear stock.)

Add the celery, onion, lemon, parsley, thyme and bay leaves. Cover the bones with the cold water and bring to a simmer. Do not bring the stock to a boil at any time or it will become cloudy.

Simmer, uncovered, for 45 minutes to 1 hour, skimming the impurities that float to the top every 10 minutes; otherwise your stock will become cloudy and bitter.

Gently remove the bones and vegetables from the stock, then strain it through a fine-mesh sieve or cheesecloth.

Quickly cool the stock and refrigerate for up to 5 days until needed. Pour any unused stock into freezer-safe containers and freeze for up to 3 months. Otherwise, the stock will keep for 3 or 4 days in the refrigerator.

> ⟋⟍ tip ⟋⟍
>
> *You can buy fish bones from your local fishmonger, but if that's not an option, you can buy fish with the bones in and freeze the bones. If you seal them in a bag, they should keep for up to 3 months in the freezer. Be sure to save the bones only from lean fish like halibut or haddock. Bones from oily fish like salmon or tuna just don't make good stock.*

lobster stock

This rich lobster stock is packed with flavour and can be used in a variety of ways. MAKES 12 CUPS (3 L)

3 lb (1.5 kg) lobster shells (from 4 to
   6 lobsters)
2 cups (500 mL) diced onion
1 cup (250 mL) medium-diced carrot
1 cup (250 mL) medium-diced celery
¼ cup (60 mL) coarsely chopped garlic
¼ cup (60 mL) tomato paste
¼ cup (60 mL) dry white wine
¼ cup (60 mL) brandy
6 quarts (6 L) cold water

Preheat the oven to 375°F (190°C).

Place the lobster shells in a roasting pan and roast for 20 to 25 minutes, turning once. Add the onion, carrot, celery, garlic and tomato paste and continue to cook for 15 minutes.

Remove the pan from the oven, transfer the shells and vegetables to a large stockpot, and deglaze the roasting pan with the wine and brandy.

Add the deglazing liquid to the stockpot.

Add the cold water. Bring to a boil, reduce the heat to a simmer and cook, uncovered, for 1 hour.

Strain the stock through a fine-mesh sieve or cheesecloth and return to the stove. Return to a boil, then reduce to a simmer again.

Allow the stock to reduce to about half its original volume, about 1 hour.

Quickly cool the stock and refrigerate for up to 3 days until needed. Pour any unused stock into freezer-safe containers and freeze for up to 3 months.

⁐ tip ⁍

You can freeze lobster shells until you need them. If you seal them in a bag, they should keep for up to 3 months in the freezer.

orange ginger glaze

Everyone should have a jar of this in his or her refrigerator. I have used this glaze for roasting almost every type of meat, and it's great for adding flavour to dressings, livening up drinks and drizzling on roasted vegetables or cheesecake. It even tastes great on ice cream. MAKES ABOUT 1 CUP (250 ML)

1 cup (250 mL) sugar
3 cups (750 mL) orange juice
¼ cup (60 mL) minced fresh young
   ginger (peeled)

Dissolve the sugar in the orange juice. Add the ginger and bring to a boil. Reduce the heat and simmer until the mixture has reduced by two-thirds, about 20 minutes, and has a thick, syrupy texture.

Be sure to skim off the impurities several times while the liquid is reducing, otherwise the glaze will become bitter.

Strain through a medium-mesh sieve into a jar to remove the ginger and refrigerate for up to 1 month. (If you really like ginger you can leave it in!)

balsamic vinaigrette

Balsamic vinaigrette is the king of vinaigrettes. I usually break out this recipe when the tomatoes are ready here on PEI. A little drizzle of this dressing over some tomatoes and Gouda makes a nice appetizer on a hot summer evening. Balsamic is sweeter than many vinegars, so it requires less oil. Try tossing this balsamic vinaigrette with fresh raspberries, cubes of havarti and spinach! MAKES 1½ CUPS (375 ML)

½ cup (125 mL) balsamic vinegar
1 clove garlic
½ bunch fresh basil
1 tsp (5 mL) Dijon mustard
1 tsp (5 mL) freshly ground black pepper
½ cup (125 mL) virgin olive oil
½ cup (125 mL) canola oil

In a blender, combine the vinegar, garlic, basil, mustard and pepper, and purée until smooth.

With the blender still running, slowly add the oils in a slow stream until fully incorporated. Transfer to a bottle or jar and refrigerate until needed.

Serve cool on your favourite greens.

citrus vinaigrette

The acidity of this dressing can be easily adjusted by adding a little more vinegar or sweetener as required. The citrus complements any salad greens you can think of and makes a nice drizzle or marinade for seafood. MAKES 1½ CUPS (375 ML)

¼ cup (60 mL) white wine vinegar
2 Tbsp (30 mL) orange juice
2 Tbsp (30 mL) lime juice
2 Tbsp (30 mL) lemon juice
2 Tbsp (30 mL) chopped chives
1 Tbsp (15 mL) chopped tarragon
2 tsp (10 mL) Dijon mustard
1 cup (250 mL) extra virgin olive oil
salt and pepper

In a bowl, combine all the ingredients except the oil, salt and pepper, and mix thoroughly.

Add the oil in a slow, steady stream, whisking constantly. Season to taste with salt and pepper.

This can be refrigerated for up to 1 week.

raspberry vinaigrette

This vinaigrette is a staple in my kitchen. I love the combination of raspberry and black pepper. It's just sweet enough to dress a bitter salad but can still go well with fruit or meats. You can substitute blueberries or strawberries for the raspberries, but I prefer not to. MAKES ABOUT 1¼ CUPS (310 ML)

1½ cups (375 mL) fresh or frozen
   (and thawed) raspberries
½ cup (125 mL) honey
2 Tbsp (30 mL) lemon juice
   or balsamic vinegar
¼ cup (60 mL) canola oil
2 tsp (10 mL) freshly ground black pepper
salt

Combine the raspberries and honey in a small saucepan. Mash them together and bring to a boil. Reduce the heat and simmer until the raspberries break down and the mixture is slightly thick. Remove from the heat and strain through a fine-mesh sieve to remove the seeds.

Transfer to a mixing bowl and whisk in the lemon juice or vinegar. Pour the oil in a stream, whisking to combine. Add the pepper and adjust the seasoning to taste.

This will keep in the refrigerator for 1 week.

maple vinaigrette

This is great for any salad, particularly for those that include chicken or pork. Use this recipe as a guide. Some people prefer their vinaigrettes more acidic, and some prefer them sweeter. Simply adjust the tartness by adding more vinegar or maple syrup according to taste. MAKES 1 CUP (250 ML)

¼ cup (60 mL) maple syrup
¼ cup (60 mL) cider vinegar
1½ tsp (7 mL) Dijon mustard
1½ tsp (7 mL) minced green onion
1 tsp (5 mL) minced garlic
¼ cup (60 mL) extra virgin olive oil
¼ cup (60 mL) vegetable oil
salt and pepper

In a bowl, combine the syrup, vinegar, mustard, green onion and garlic. Slowly add the oils in a steady stream, whisking constantly. Taste and adjust seasoning with salt and pepper.

honey dijon dressing

This is a nice, light dressing that goes well with any bitter green or fruit-based salad. I often have it on a hot day with arugula, cottage cheese and fresh straw-berries. It keeps well in the refrigerator and has a little bit of a kick. MAKES ABOUT 1 CUP (250 ML)

½ cup (125 mL) honey
¼ cup (60 mL) lemon juice
2 tsp (10 mL) Dijon mustard
1 tsp (5 mL) grainy mustard
2 tsp (10 mL) minced fresh tarragon
1 clove garlic (minced)
¼ cup (60 mL) virgin olive oil
salt and pepper

Combine the honey, lemon juice, mustards, tarragon and garlic in a bowl and whisk until well combined. Slowly whisk in the oil until incorporated and season to taste with salt and pepper.

If you refrigerate this dressing, you will have to remove it from the refrigerator 15 minutes before using it to bring it to room temperature, then shake and recombine it.

This is also good as a light vegetable dip.

sour cream and herb dressing

This is a great basic ranch-style dressing that can be used for salads, dipping or flavouring other dishes (like mashed potatoes!). You can mix it up by chang-ing the type and amount of herbs or adding other savoury elements like ginger or lemongrass. MAKES ABOUT 1 CUP (250 ML)

½ cup (125 mL) low-fat sour cream
¼ cup (60 mL) mayonnaise (low-fat
   if you prefer)
1 clove garlic (minced)
1 Tbsp (15 mL) minced fresh basil
1 Tbsp (15 mL) minced fresh tarragon
1 Tbsp (15 mL) minced fresh parsley
1 Tbsp (15 mL) lemon juice
1 tsp (5 mL) freshly ground black pepper
¼ cup (60 mL) water

Combine all the ingredients except the water in a bowl, whisking until smooth. Add the water slowly until the desired texture is reached.

If you're using this recipe as a dip, omit the water or it will be too thin to cling to the vegetables.

This keeps in the refrigerator for 10 days.

simple syrup

Simple syrup is good to have in the fridge for cocktails, cakes, fruit coulis, dessert sauces—anytime you require liquid sweetness. It can be flavoured with all sorts of ingredients like amaretto, kirsch, rum or vanilla, making it quite a handy recipe to know. You can find glucose in syrup form at cake-decorating stores; it's used in this recipe to control crystallization. MAKES 5 CUPS (1.25 L)

4 cups (1 L) water
1⅓ lb (600 g) sugar
1 cup (250 mL) glucose

In a medium-sized saucepan, combine all the ingredients. Bring to a boil and then cool. Transfer the simple syrup to an airtight glass jar and refrigerate. Keeps for up to 2 months.

pastry cream

Keep this versatile staple in the refrigerator. It's great in trifle and fruit flans, or as a filling for many classic cakes, such as Boston cream pie or Paris-Brest. If you want a lighter pastry cream, just fold in some whipped cream. MAKES 4 CUPS (2 L)

1 cup (250 mL) sugar
¼ cup (60 mL) cornstarch
3 eggs
½ tsp (2 mL) vanilla extract
4 cups (1 L) 2% milk
⅓ cup (80 mL) unsalted butter (softened)

Combine the sugar and cornstarch. Add the eggs one at a time to form a paste. Add the vanilla.

Bring the milk to a boil. Add the cornstarch mix and cook, stirring, until the mixture has returned to a boil. Continue for cook for 2 minutes, stirring constantly.

Remove from the heat. Add the butter and transfer to a bowl to cool. Sprinkle a little bit of sugar overtop to prevent a skin from forming.

Serve warm or cool. If serving cool, cover and refrigerate for up to 1 week.

egg wash

Egg wash is a kitchen essential. It can be used to brush on pastries to help with the browning, to stick pastries together or when you want breadcrumbs to stick onto something. MAKES ABOUT ½ CUP (125 ML)

  2 whole eggs
  2 Tbsp (30 mL) 2% milk

Place the ingredients in a mixing bowl and beat until smooth.

streusel topping

This topping can be used in a variety of products to add a sweet crunch to your baked goods. Do not overmix. This is one recipe where it is better if the end product is lumpy. MAKES ENOUGH TO TOP 1 PIE

  ¾ cup (185 mL) all-purpose flour
  ½ cup (125 mL) brown sugar (packed)
  ½ cup (125 mL) unsalted butter
  ½ tsp (2 mL) cinnamon

Place all the ingredients in a bowl and mix until combined. Do not overmix. Leave some lumps.

hazelnut chocolate mousse

Every good cook needs a reliable chocolate mousse recipe. This one is awesome! Try a dollop or two in a specialty coffee, or serve it as part of a sexy dessert—it pairs well with just about anything sweet.

It's definitely something that you should master so that you can produce it at a moment's notice. SERVES 4—6

  ½ lb (250 g) hazelnut chocolate
    (or milk chocolate)
  ⅓ cup (80 mL) unsalted butter (softened)
  2 Tbsp (30 mL) Frangelico
  4 egg whites
  2 Tbsp (30 mL) sugar
  1 cup (250 mL) whipping cream
  1 tsp (5 mL) vanilla extract

In a double boiler melt together the chocolate, butter and Frangelico. Let cool slightly.

Whip the egg whites with the sugar until stiff peaks form.

In a separate bowl, whip the cream and vanilla until stiff peaks form.

Fold the egg whites into the chocolate mixture very gently and then fold in the whipped cream. Cover and refrigerate until the mixture has set, about 1 hour.

Pipe with a piping bag or dollop in individual serving bowls. Serve with fresh berries, bananas or oranges. Garnish with shaved chocolate and whipped cream.

banana loaf

This is a family favourite, as we always have overripe bananas in the freezer—the mushier the better. Enjoy a slice with some butter. Or lightly butter both sides and fry in a pan, flipping once to brown both sides. Serve it with some sliced banana and a scoop of your favourite vanilla ice cream. Yummy!—J.M. SERVES 4—6

1 cup (250 mL) unsalted butter (softened)

3 cups (750 mL) sugar

4 eggs

3 cups (750 mL) mashed banana
   (5 to 6 bananas)

½ cup (125 mL) buttermilk
   (or 1½ tsp/7.5 mL vinegar with milk
   to make ½ cup/125 mL)

1½ tsp (7.5 mL) vanilla extract

4½ cups (1.125 L) all-purpose flour

1 Tbsp (15 mL) baking powder

1½ tsp (7.5 mL) baking soda

½ tsp (2 mL) salt

½ cup (125 mL) chopped walnuts (optional)

½ cup (125 mL) shredded sweetened
   coconut (optional)

Preheat the oven to 350°F (180°C). Grease a large 9- × 5-inch (2 L) loaf pan with butter.

Cream the butter and sugar and add the eggs one at a time, beating well between each addition until fully incorporated. Next add the banana, buttermilk and vanilla.

In a separate bowl, combine the flour, baking powder, baking soda and salt.

Add the dry ingredients to the banana, vanilla and buttermilk mixture in 3 additions. Fold in the nuts and coconut if using.

Transfer the batter to the prepared pan and bake for 18 to 20 minutes. The loaf is ready when a toothpick inserted in the centre comes out clean.

Turn the loaf out of the pan and cool on a baking rack. This loaf is best served warm.

acknowledgements

Many thanks to my (Jeff's) grandmother Leona McCourt for fostering my love of blueberries! This was truly the beginning of our book.

Thank you to Tracey Singleton for helping us bring our "baby" into this world, even when you were doing the same, times three! You believed in us from the beginning.

Thanks to Chef Michael Smith for the advice, the chats and the endorsement of our book.

Thanks to Berni Wood for cracking the whip when it needed to be cracked!

Thanks to James Ingram, truly one of Canada's great photographers! Your photos bring our stories to life.

Thanks to Patti Hetherington for her amazing food and prop styling. You really got us, Patti.

We would also like to acknowledge and thank our partners, who are committed to advancing Prince Edward Island's culinary products:

Atlantic Canada Opportunities Agency (ACOA)
 (www.acoa.ca)
Tourism Prince Edward Island
 (www.gentleisland.com)
PEI Department of Agriculture
PEI Department of Fisheries, Aquaculture &
 Rural Development
PEI Culinary Alliance (www.peiflavours.ca)
Red Shores Racetrack and Casino
 (www.redshores.ca)
Olde Towne Orchard
 (www.oldetowneorchard.com)

Clam Diggers Beach House and Restaurant
 (www.clamdiggers.ca)
Prince Edward Aqua Farms (www.peaqua.com)
Amalgamated Dairies Limited (www.ADL.ca)
The Culinary Institute of Canada and Holland
 College (www.hollandcollege.com)

Thanks to the fellow members of the PEI Association of Chefs and Cooks who contributed recipes and shared their passion: Mike Eyolfson, Brian Thomson, Hans Anderegg, Kevin Boyce, Richard Braunauer, Pam Good, Kimball Bernard, Hans Wicki, Joerg Soltermann, Michael Bryanton, Linda Hellingman, Rob O'Connor, Bob Miller, Andrew Morrison, Ted Grant, Andrew Nicholson, Blair Zinck, Paul Peters, Shirleen Peardon, Patrick Young, Mark Gregory, Alex Wilman, Mike Smith, Jeff Malone, Irwin MacKinnon, Domenic Serio, Ryan MacIssac and Norman Day.

Thanks to Paderno for your continued support for whatever project we tackle. It does not go unnoticed!

Thank you to Elaine Black for your constant support and for holding the rudder that helped keep the ship sailing.

Thanks, Don Taylor and Arlene Smith, for letting me (Austin) be part of Clam Diggers and loaning us the beach for our clambake. And, Adam Loo, you really can cook, man!

Thank you to the Lewis family—Chad, Lori-Anne, Thomas, Jodi, Morgan, Katelyn and Sydney— who showed us what family farming really is on Toad Hill.

Thanks to the Cheese Lady, Martina Terbeek, for sharing your love for cheese.

Thanks to Kenny Mutch for sharing all that Riverview Market has to offer. Love that bacon!

Thanks to David Cole for organizing the boat for our mussel tour.

Thanks to Joey Gauthier, captain of the *Julie Ann Jamie*, Ian Gauthier, captain of the *Aly Dan*, and Doug Doiron, of Doiron Fisheries, for providing the boats, lobsters, traps, gear and the whole lobster experience. Thanks for making it special.

Thanks to Mike Whitty for taking the time to talk cranberries.

Thanks to the Artz family, especially little Anthony, for welcoming us to your farm.

Thanks to Christine Farkas for formatting all the recipes.

Thanks to Johnny Flynn and his daughter Sarah at Colville Bay Oysters—even though my (Jeff's) shoes nearly floated away!

Thanks to John Rossignol at Rossignol Estate Winery. Your dedication is an inspiration!

Thanks to Edwin McKie for meeting us so early in the blueberry field on such short notice!

Thanks to Lee Gallant and the crew of the *Gulf Cruiser* for the tuna tail!

Thanks to Chef Hans Anderegg for sharing one of your secret mushroom spots and for being a mentor and friend to us all!

To all the local champions on this great Island of ours—keep it up! Spread the word and always choose to support local producers!

To learn more about Prince Edward Island's culinary scene, visit www.peiflavours.ca.

And thanks to everyone who bought this book! We hope you enjoy *Flavours of Prince Edward Island*.
—Jeff, Austin and Allan

index